<INSERT COVER>
COVER DESIGN IS NOT YET
APPROVED

SUCCEEDING IN FLORIDA'S
SMALL CLAIMS COURTS
WITHOUT A LAWYER

SUCCEEDING IN FLORIDA'S SMALL CLAIMS COURTS WITHOUT A LAWYER

BY KURT E. LEE, ESQ.
& TIM W. SOBCZAK, ESQ.

ISBN: 1500499307
ISBN 13: 9781500499303
Library of Congress Control Number: 2014912605
CreateSpace Independent Publishing Platform
North Charleston, South Carolina

DISCLAIMER OF LIABILITY

TABLE OF CONTENTS

INTRODUCTION

In Florida, "*small claims court*" is not a courthouse or even a courtroom. It describes a "*division*" within Florida's county courts and refers to a simplified procedure for resolving civil disputes involving relatively small amounts of money.[1] Although small claims court is simpler and more informal than regular civil court proceedings, there are rules that must be followed and requirements that must met. Both of which require a certain level of expertise.

This book is intended to provide individuals and businesses with the know-how to successfully navigate a Florida small claims dispute without a lawyer. It provides a full breakdown of the small claims process — from initial demand letter to the satisfaction of a judgment. It outlines the special rules of procedure that pertain to small claims proceedings and offers suggestions for success. Finally, this book provides the forms small claims litigants will need to move forward.

Because small claims court is a judicial proceeding, there will be legal jargon with which one needs to become familiar.[2] For example, the "*parties*" or "*litigants*" in a small claims case are sometimes more particularly referred to as "*plaintiffs*" and "*defendants*." A "*plaintiff*" is an

---

[1] *See LaSalla v. Pools by George of Pinellas County, Inc.*, 125 So. 2d 1016 (Fla. 2d DCA 2013) ("These rules do not create a 'small claims court.' They simply create rules of procedure for use in county court when the amount in controversy is small."); Maryanne Morse, Seminole County Clerk of Court, What Is Small Claims Court?, www.seminole-clerk.org/FeesAndForms (last visited January 10, 2014).

[2] There are many online dictionaries which can help with legal terms. One resource which might be of assistance is http://www.nolo.com/dictionary.

individual or business filing or initiating the lawsuit and a "*defendant*" is an individual or business responding to the claims being made.

Because small claims court is a judicial proceeding, there are also formal rules that direct the procedures and events that occur in the lawsuit. The procedural rules that govern a small claims case are known as the Florida Small Claims Rules.[3] This book will reference specific rules of the Florida Small Claims Rules by using the abbreviation "Fla. Sm. Cl. R."

In short, whether one is a plaintiff or a defendant (or anticipates being a plaintiff or defendant) in a small claims case, this book will help him succeed in Florida's small claims courts. No attorney representation necessary.

---

[3] The Florida Small Claims Rules as of December 1, 2013, are included in this book. You should check for updates at http://www.floridabar.org/tfb/TFBLegalRes.nsf/

1

FLORIDA'S SMALL CLAIMS COURT

Until 1973, Florida had more kinds of trial courts than any state except New York. Thankfully, a movement developed in the late 1960s to reform this confusing system. Florida now has a simple two-tiered trial court system made up of "*circuit*" courts and "*county*" courts.

In Florida, county courts have assigned jurisdiction over disputes involving damages up to $15,000.[1] A small claims case—where the amount of money involved is $5,000 or less, not including costs, prejudgment interest, and attorneys' fees[2]—falls under this umbrella. Larger claims may find themselves in circuit courts, which have general trial jurisdiction over matters that have not been assigned to the county courts by the Florida legislature.[3]

The basic goal of the small claims process is to enable people and businesses to resolve minor civil disputes through the court system without having to go through formal and complex court procedures. Indeed, small claims court is the only legal proceeding where a business may represent itself without having to hire an attorney.[4]

---

[1] § 34.01(1)(c), Fla. Stat. (2013).

[2] Fla. Sm. Cl. R. 7.010(b).

[3] Florida State Courts, Brief Description of Circuit Courts in Florida, http://www.flcourts.org/courts/circuit/cir_description.shtml (last visited January 10, 2014).

[4] Fla. Sm. Cl. R. 7.050(a)(2).

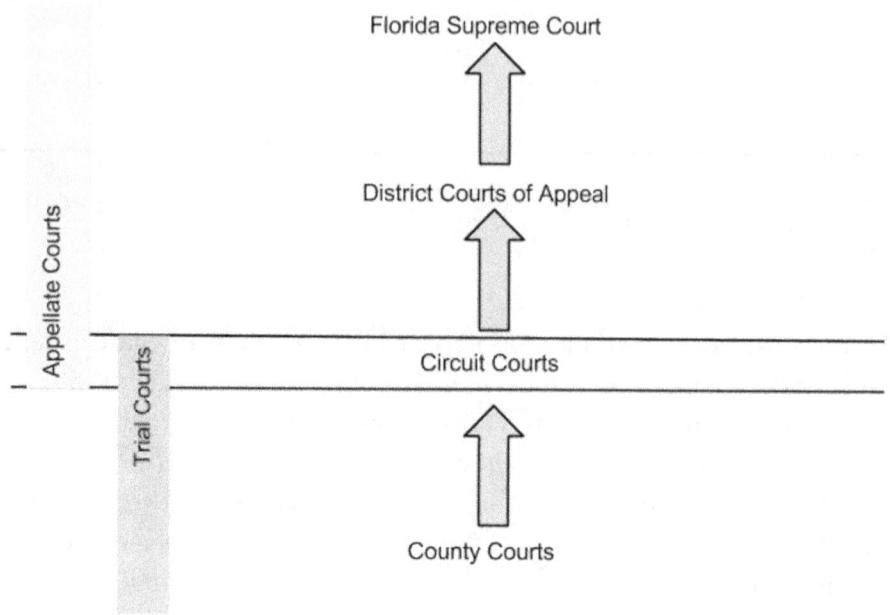

An Overview of Florida's Current Court Structure

2

WHO CAN FILE A
SMALL CLAIMS CASE

Any person who is at least 18 years old may file a small claims case. A minor may also sue in small claims court, but a parent or guardian needs to file the case on his behalf. It is not necessary to hire a lawyer to file the case. In fact, it is often said that small claims court is a "people's court."[5]

Filing as an Individual: A person may be able to file a small claims case even if he lacks the ability to pay the associated filing fees. A person seeking to be excused from paying filing fees (and, also, from paying the costs associated with service of process) based upon an inability to pay must apply to the Clerk of the Court for a determination of civil indigent status using an application form provided by the Clerk's office.[6]

Filing as a Business: A business, whether owned by an individual, a partnership, or a corporation, may also file a lawsuit in small claims court. A corporation in a small claims action does not need to hire a lawyer to file its case nor to represent it. A corporation may

---

[5] Small claims courts are designed to be "a People's Court in which technical rules of pleading must not obscure the greater purpose of justice for all." *Donoghue v. Wallach,* 455 So.2d 1085, 1086 n.1 (Fla. 2d DCA 1984).

[6] *See* § 57.082, Fla. Stat. (2013).

be represented by an officer of the corporation, or any employee authorized in writing by an officer of the corporation.[7]

---

[7] Fla. Sm. Cl. R. 7.050(a)(2). Also, though not necessarily required, the Florida Small Claims Rules provide a form for establishing the corporate officer's authority to represent the corporation in the case. *See* Fla. Sm. Cl. R. Form 7.350.

3

WHO SHOULD FILE A SMALL CLAIMS CASE

If someone owes money and will not repay it or if someone has property and will not return it, the person or business owed the money or owning the property may be able to resolve the problem through small claims court.[8] But, before filing a small claims case, every potential plaintiff should answer the following questions:

1. Is the amount of money in dispute or the property at issue worth $5,000 or less?

Florida's small claims court procedures only apply to cases where the amount of money or property in dispute has a value equal to or less than $5,000. If a potential plaintiff is seeking *more* than $5,000, or relief that is "equitable" in nature (e.g., an injunction or to foreclose upon a lien), then the claim must be filed in county court or, possibly, circuit court.[9]

---

[8] Maryanne Morse, Seminole County Clerk of Court, *supra* note 1

[9] Remember: Florida's small claims courts are a division within and a part of the state's county courts. The direction to file claims seeking more than $5,000 in damages or relief other than money in "county court" might be better stated as a direction to *not* file such a claim in the county court's small claims division.

2. Is there a valid legal claim against the other party?
Obviously it would be unwise to file a small claims case and incur the costs associated with a court filing without a valid legal claim. Florida law is very broad. If a potential plaintiff has any uncertainty about the existence of a claim or its validity, it may be helpful to talk to an attorney before filing a small claims case.

3. Is it possible to get the necessary evidence to prove the claim in court?
The party filing a small claims case may be "right" but that does not mean that it's possible to prove the case at trial. Generally speaking, if a party is asserting a claim he needs to support it with witness testimony (which might be only the party's own testimony) and through documents (invoices, contracts, emails, etc.). Without proof, the claim will not be successful; "right" has nothing to do with it.

It can be difficult to cause people to appear as witnesses and to repeat before a judge something that may have been said. It can be difficult to obtain documents, particularly if they need to come from a person or business outside of the state of Florida. All of these things need to be taken into consideration before filing a small claims case. A potential plaintiff should evaluate who can and will testify and obtain the location of the documents needed to prove the case. It might be helpful to talk to an attorney before filing a case and to get some advice about the evidence needed to prove a claim.

4. Can the correct legal name and address of the potential defendants be ascertained?[10]
This sounds like a silly question but it can be difficult to correctly identify whom the defendant should be. This

---

[10] *See, e.g.,* Flagler County Clerk of Court, Small Claims, http://www.flaglerclerk.com/courtsmallclaims.htm (last visited January 10, 2014).

is particularly true in matters involving independent contractors or fictitious names. A plaintiff must be able to identify and "*serve*" the defendant with the statement of claim. If a plaintiff cannot locate a defendant, then the lawsuit will never get off the ground.

5. Is the dispute such that it merits the expenditure of a few hundred dollars and, potentially, a significant amount of time in court proceedings?

6. Lawsuits often last longer than people think. A potential plaintiff should expect the action to take several months to resolve and hours of time preparing the necessary documents and appearing in court. It comes down to Time versus Money. If a potential plaintiff's time is worth more than the amount in dispute, it may be wise to forego a lawsuit.

7. Finally and most importantly, have all possible and reasonable means to amicably resolve the problem been attempted?[11]

8. Legal action should be a last resort. Potential plaintiffs should try to talk to the other party or parties about the matter before filing a lawsuit. It is possible that emotions have cooled or previously unknown facts have now come to light. It is worth trying to resolve all disputes on a cordial basis.

Indeed, potential plaintiffs might try to give the other party a reason to amicably resolve a matter and avoid small claims action entirely. Potential plaintiffs might offer to

---

[11] Superior Court of California, County of Contra Costa, How to Settle A Dispute, http://cc-courthelp.org/index.cfm?fuseaction=Page.ViewPage&pageId=4757, (last visited January 10, 2014).

accept less than the full amount owed in exchange for a prompt payment or propose a payment plan. Many potential defendants realize that it makes sense to pay more than they believe is owed to end a dispute and to avoid the possibility of being saddled with court costs and interest in addition to the principal amount of the debt. Settling the matter out of court spares both parties' time, energy, and ultimately their money.

Potential plaintiffs might also consider sending the other person or business a short, clear letter demanding payment or the return of their property. Even if the demand letter fails to resolve the matter and avoid the necessity of filing a small claims case, a potential plaintiff's exercise in writing out his case in a careful, business-like manner is good practice for later telling the story in a careful, business-like manner to the judge. In addition, a pre-suit demand letter might help demonstrate to the judge or jury later how the lawsuit was filed as a last resort.

If the answers to the above questions are all "yes," then it may make sense to file a small claims lawsuit to resolve the dispute.

4

WHERE TO FILE A
SMALL CLAIMS CASE

Small claims cases should be filed with the clerk of court in the appropriate county, i.e., the appropriate "*venue*" —addresses for all of Florida's Clerks of Court are set forth at the end of this book. Clerks' offices are busy places, but they will usually have directions to or signage for a window or a line that has been designated for small claims cases.

The clerk will charge a filing fee when the case is filed.[12]

It is important to file the small claims case in an appropriate county. Indeed, county court judges are instructed in the small claims rules to consider whether an action was filed in a proper venue prior to entering judgment.[13] If a case is filed in an incorrect venue, the judge may dismiss the case or enter an order transferring the case to another county. If the case is dismissed, the plaintiff will need to pay filing fees again when he re-files the case in the proper county.

---

[12] "Filing fees for small claims actions are established in the Florida Statutes and local county ordinances, and are subject to change by legislative action." Florida State Courts, Small Claims, http://www.flcourts.org/gen_public/family/self_help/small-claims.shtml, (last visited January 10, 2014).

[13] *See Tax Certificate Judgments, Inc. v. Wright*, 826 So. 2d 1051 (Fla. 4th DCA 2002)("In transferring venue on her own, the county judge did exactly what rule 7.170 contemplates, and the circuit court, in affirming, applied the correct law.").

A proper location[14] to file a small claims case may be in a county:

1. Where the contract was entered.

2. If the case is on an unsecured promissory note, where the note was signed or where the maker resides.

3. If the case is to recover property or to foreclose a lien, where the property is located.

4. Where the event giving rise to the case occurred.

5. Where any one or more of the defendants sued reside. (To find out where a corporation "*resides*," you can search the Florida Division of Corporations' Sunbiz web site - www.sunbiz.org.)

6. Any location agreed to in a contract.

7. In an action for money due, if there is no agreement as to where a case may be filed, where payment is to be made. If, however, the action is based upon an unsecured promissory note, then proper venue is, as aforementioned, the county where the note was signed by the maker or in which the maker resides.[15]

There may be—and often is—more than one appropriate county in which venue would be proper. For example, if there are multiple defendants to an action, a plaintiff may choose any county in which any defendant may be considered a resident, without consideration of

---

[14] *See generally* Ch. 47, Fla. Stat. (2013).

[15] *Foster v. Greco*, 320 So. 2d 43, 44 (Fla. 4th DCA 1975).

the co-defendants.[16] This is an opportunity for strategy and a plaintiff should, therefore, give some thought to where his case will be filed. The best practice is for a plaintiff to choose the county that is most convenient for his witnesses as opposed to trying to select the most inconvenient county for a defendant.

A potential plaintiff who is unsure about where to file his small claims case should consider consulting with an attorney. An attorney consultation would also be helpful if a potential defendant resides in another state or if the small claims case involves an event that occurred in another state.

---

[16] *Brown v. Nagelhout*, 84 So. 3d 304, 311 (Fla. 2012).

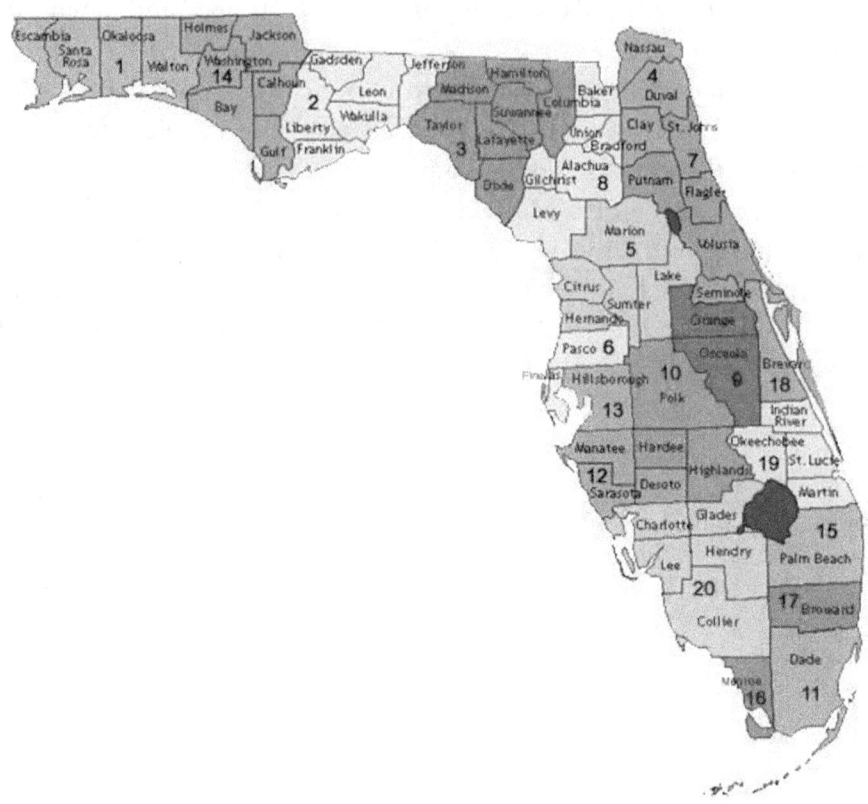

Map of Florida's Counties With Judicial Circuit Numbers

5

THE STATEMENT OF CLAIM

All small claims cases start with a *"Statement of Claim."*[17] A statement of claim is the paper on which a plaintiff writes the reasons why a defendant is subject to liability and for what the defendant is liable. A small claims case is commenced when a plaintiff files a statement of claim and thereby informs each defendant of the basis and the amount of each claim.

A statement of claim is a formal document, and Florida's Small Claims Rules prescribe what it needs to include. Adhering to those requirements can help ensure the process moves forward smoothly. It is often helpful to review a blank statement of claim form to ensure that all necessary information is included. Blank statement of claim forms may be found at the clerk's offices in the county where the small claims case is being filed, and some clerks have statement of claim forms available online.[18]

The clerk's offices, at a plaintiff's request, will help prepare the statement of claim and any other documents that may be required to start a small claims case.[19] The clerk will provide the case number and, in some counties, identify the division or judge to which the case is

---

[17] Fla. Sm. Cl. R. 7.050(a)(1).

[18] For example, the Palm Beach County Clerk of Court's website permits users to complete small claims forms online at http://www.mypalmbeachclerk.com/selfservice. For another example, the Pinellas County Clerk of Court provides forms with blanks which may be completed online at http://www.pinellasclerk.org/aspinclude2/ASPInclude. asp?pageName=smclaimsforms.htm.

[19] Fla. Sm. Cl. R. 7.050(c).

assigned. Although the clerk will assist with preparing the statement of claim, it is the plaintiff's responsibility to complete and sign the form and state a legal basis for the claim.[20]

A model statement of claim form follows on the next page.[21]

---

[20] Fla. Sm. Cl. R. 7.050(a)(2).

[21] The link to the Alachua County Clerk of Courts' forms: http://www.alachuacounty.us/Depts/Clerk/Pages/Forms.aspx

THE STATEMENT OF CLAIM

**IN THE COUNTY COURT OF THE EIGHTH JUDICIAL CIRCUIT,
IN AND FOR ALACHUA COUNTY, FLORIDA**
201 East University Avenue
Gainesville Florida 32601
(352) 374-3636

_____
PLAINTIFF

_____
Address

_____
Phone

- vs -

_____
DEFENDANT

_____
Address

_____
Phone

Case No.: _____

Division: _____

_____
DEFENDANT

_____
Address

_____
Phone

STATEMENT CLAIM
(General)

Plaintiff(s), _____,

sue(s) Defendant(s),_____ and alleges:

_____

_____

_____

_____

_____

_____

If a Defendant is to be served with process outside the State of Florida, see Exhibit "A", attached.

WHEREFORE, Plaintiff(s) demands judgment for damages against defendant(s) in the amount of $_____ principal, plus $_____ interest, plus $_____ service charge, plus $_____ court costs.

_____
PLAINTIFF(S)

Blank Statement of Claim Form from Alachua County Clerk of Court

-- 15 --

6

IDENTIFYING THE PARTIES

A plaintiff needs to identify the proper parties in the statement of claim. The names, addresses, and telephone numbers, including area code, of all parties—or their attorneys, if any—must be stated on the statement of claim.[22] The parties' names, addresses, and phone numbers are usually contained in the "*caption*" or "*style*" of the case — the portion of the statement of claim above the document's title.

A sample caption is as follows:

IN THE COUNTY COURT IN AND FOR SARASOTA COUNTY, FLORIDA
SMALL CLAIMS DIVISION

PAINTING BY JOE, INC.
123 Main Street
Sarasota, FL 34230
(941) 121-5555
      Plaintiff,

v.   Case No. 123-CC-4562

HARRY HOMEOWNER
456 Residential Way
Sarasota, FL 34231
(941) 555-1212
      Defendant.

_____/

---

[22] Fla. Sm. Cl. R. 7.050(b).

Being sure to properly identify all of the parties sounds like a rather obvious requirement, but it is very important that the plaintiffs and the defendants are properly identified in a statement of claim. The time spent researching the proper and current names of the parties to a case may make a difference in whether a plaintiff is able to recover damages should a judgment be entered in his favor. Needless to say, it's worth the extra effort.

If after filing a statement of claim a plaintiff discovers he has improperly named a party — e.g., named "Taylor Creek Marina, a Florida Corporation" when the correct name is "Taylor Creek Marina of Ft. Pierce, Inc." — a plaintiff should immediately file a motion asking the court to amend the statement of claim.

Corporations as Parties

Under Florida law, a corporation is treated like a person. A corporation may own property in its name, buy and sell property, and bring and defend lawsuits. In small claims cases, a corporation may be represented at any stage of the proceedings by an officer of the corporation, or any employee authorized in writing by an officer of the corporation.[23]

If a corporation is a plaintiff or a defendant, care must be taken to properly identify the name of the corporation. The name of a corporation may be verified by contacting the Florida Department of State, Division of Corporations, at (850) 488-9000 or by searching for the corporation at www.sunbiz.org. A plaintiff suing a corporation will also want to identify the corporation's *"registered agent."* (The importance of the registered agent information will be explained later in connection with *"service of process."*)

---

[23] If a corporation, whether it is a plaintiff or a defendant, opts to be represented by an officer or another authorized employee, it should file a form substantially similar to the one found here - http://www.pinellasclerk.org/aspinclude2/SmClaimsPdfs/AutCorOf. pdf.

After obtaining the corporation's proper name, its registered agent's name, and the registered agent's address, a plaintiff will identify the corporation as a defendant like this:

ABC Business, Inc.
Served through Alfred Baker, as Registered Agent
1 Main Street
Tampa, Florida 32749
(123) 456-7890

Partnerships as Parties

Partnerships are treated a little differently than a corporation.

A *"general"* partnership is an association of two or more persons who carry on as co-owners of a business.

A *"limited"* partnership is a business entity having one or more general partners and one or more limited partners. The name of a limited partnership may be verified by contacting the Florida Department of State, Division of Corporations, at (850) 488-9000 or by searching for the limited partnership at www.sunbiz.org.

When bringing a case against a general partnership, all of the responsible partners should be named as defendants.[24] An example of a general partnership listed as a defendant:

John Smith and Carl Jones d/b/a Fantastic Cleaners
15 Second Street
Miami, Florida 33313
(123) 456-7890

---

[24] "Florida follows the common law rule that a partnership cannot sue or be sued in its partnership name because it has no identity apart from its members and is not a person, either natural or artificial." *Irwindale Co., N.V. v. Three Islands Olympus*, 474 So. 2d 406, 407 (Fla. 4th DCA 1985)(quoting *Malibu Partners, Ltd. v. Schooley*, 372 So. 2d 179, 180 (Fla. 2d DCA 1979)).

When it comes to serving the statement of claim upon the general partners, a plaintiff will need a separate notice of appearance for each general partner.

When bringing a case against a limited partnership, only the limited partnership needs to be identified. Suing a limited partnership is similar to suing a corporation: a plaintiff should identify the limited partnership's correct name, registered agent, and registered agent's address via the Florida Department of State, Division of Corporations. An example of a limited partnership listed as a defendant:

Main Street Holdings, Ltd.
Served through Alfred Baker, as Registered Agent
22 Main Street
Tallahassee, Florida 33213
(123) 456-7890

Individuals and Sole Proprietorships as Parties

Just as it is important to properly identify business parties, it is important to properly identify individuals. An individual's proper name should be used; nicknames should not be used. If an individual is "doing business as" a fictitious name, then the person's name and the fictitious name should be used. A person "doing business as" a business name is sometimes referred to as a "sole proprietorship." An example of a sole proprietorship listed as a defendant:

Peter Duffy d/b/a Duffy's Remodeling
45 Main Street
Bradenton, Florida 32749
(123) 456-7890

Individuals and Businesses Using Fictitious Names as Parties

There's a pattern here: fictitious names can make it very difficult to identify a party. This is particularly true when names of businesses do not reflect who owns the business. For example, "Fantastic Cleaners" is a name that does not disclose whether it is a corporation, partnership, or something else. People and businesses doing business under a fictitious name are required to register the fictitious name with the Florida Department of State, Division of Corporations. A plaintiff seeking to identify the owner of a fictitious name may call the Division of Corporations at (850) 488-9000 or research fictitious names at www. sunbiz.org. Once a fictitious name is identified, the owner of such name should be named as the party to the lawsuit using the appropriate model set forth above.

Stating a Legal Claim

After identifying the parties to the case, the statement of claim needs a brief, clear, concise explanation of the facts and circumstances that pertain to the case.[25] The statement of claim must inform the defendant of the basis and the amount of the claim.[26] If the claim is based upon a written document, a copy of the document, or at least the pertinent part of the document, must be attached to the statement of claim.[27]

A statement of claim should be written so that it expresses a "*cause of action.*"

A "*cause of action*" is the technical term for the set of facts that will subject a defendant to liability in court. Not every wrong gives rise to a legally recognized right to recovery: one must suffer a legally recognized wrong to have the right to sue and recover damages. Each cause of action consists of the elements a plaintiff must prove before a court might enter a judgment in favor of a plaintiff. A cause of action

---

[25] Fla. Sm. Cl. R. 7.050(a)(1).

[26] *Id.*

[27] *Id.*

may be based upon the common law[28] or upon a law passed by the state or federal legislature.

An example of a common law cause of action is an action for breach of contract. To recover damages from a defendant for breaching a contract, a plaintiff must prove all of the following:[29]

1 The plaintiff and the defendant entered into a contract;

2. The plaintiff did all, or substantially all, of the essential things that the contract required him to do (or the plaintiff may prove that he was excused from doing those things);

3. All conditions required by the contract for the defendant's performance have occurred;

4. The defendant failed to do something essential which the contract required him to do (or the defendant did something which the contract prohibited him from doing and that prohibition was essential to the contract); and,

5. The plaintiff was harmed by that failure.

A plaintiff preparing a statement of claim based upon a breach of contract should draft the statement of claim in such a way to ensure that each of these elements is clearly stated. By writing the statement of claim in this manner, a plaintiff is providing himself with a roadmap for the trial because he will need to prove all of the elements of his cause of action at trial to recover a judgment. If a plaintiff is using a statement of claim form, he will include these

---

[28] The "common law" is that portion of the law which is derived from custom and judicial precedent rather than statutes.

[29] *See generally In re Standard Jury Instructions--Contract & Bus. Cases*, 116 So. 3d 284, 306 (Fla. 2013).

elements in the blanks provided for an explanation of the details of the claim.

An example of a statement of claim based upon a breach of contract, which includes the elements described above and which will ultimately need to be proven at trial, is as follows:

STATEMENT OF CLAIM

Plaintiff, Painting By Joe, Inc., sues Defendant, Harry Homeowner, and alleges:

Plaintiff and Defendant entered into a written contract, a copy of which is attached as Exhibit "A." Plaintiff painted Defendant's garage floor as required by the contract, but Defendant failed to pay Plaintiff the agreed upon amount of $500.00 for Plaintiff's work. There is now due, owing, and unpaid from Defendant to Plaintiff $500.00, plus interest on the unpaid sum. All conditions precedent to this action have occurred or been waived.

WHEREFORE, Plaintiff demands judgment for damages against Defendant.

A sample statement of claim form from the Walton County Clerk of Court follows. To state the aforementioned claim for a breach of contract using this form, a plaintiff might "check" the blank associated with "Money due" for labor and materials furnished and then write his claim in the "Additional Information" portion of the form.

KURT E. LEE, ESQ. & TIM W. SOBCZAK, ESQ.

IN THE COUNTY COURT IN AND FOR WALTON COUNTY, FLORIDA
SUMMARY CLAIMS DIVISION

CASE NO.: _____

_____   vs.   _____
_____   _____
Plaintiff(s)   Defendant(s)
_____   _____
Address, City, State, Zip   Address, City, State, Zip
(___) _____   (___) _____
Phone #   Phone #

STATEMENT OF CLAIM

Plaintiff claims these amounts $_____ Principal
to be due from defendant(s) for $_____ Interest
the reasons set forth below: $_____ Court Costs

                                        $_____ TOTAL

_____ Money due Plaintiff on open account. (See attached copy of accounts.).

_____ Money due Plaintiff on accounts stated and agreed to between them or following business transactions between
them; Plaintiff rendered a statement to Defendant who did not object. (See attached copy of state of accounts.).

_____ Money loaned by Plaintiff to Defendant on _____ with interest thereon since
_____. (Loan agreement attached.)

_____ Money due Plaintiff for labor and materials furnished to Defendant. (List time, materials and charges below.)

_____ Rent due Plaintiff for certain premises. (List below: address of premises and amount of rent past due, and attach
copy of any written lease.)

_____ Other: (Explain below.) Additional Information: _____
_____
_____

STATE OF FLORIDA
COUNTY OF WALTON
Under penalties of perjury and upon my oath, I state that the facts contained in this statement are true and correct, and the
Defendant is/is not in the military service. If corporate Plaintiff, the undersigned is an officer or an employee authorized by an officer
of the corporation to represent it in this proceeding.

_____   _____
Plaintiff(s)   Office Held

Sworn to and subscribed before me this _____ day of _____, 20_____.

ALEX ALFORD   By: _____
Walton County Clerk of the Circuit Court   Deputy Clerk or Notary Public
and County Comptroller

-- 24 --

7

Examples of Legal Claims A/K/A Causes of Action

An example of a cause of action based upon a law passed by the Florida Legislature is an action for damages based upon a violation of the Florida Consumer Collection Practices Act, sections 559.55 - 559.785, Florida Statutes (2013). The Florida Consumer Collection Practices Act prohibits a number of consumer collection debt practices. To recover damages from a defendant for violating this Act's prohibition against a person collecting a consumer debt by using or threatening the use of violence, a plaintiff must prove all of the following:

1. The defendant was a person as defined by section 559.55, Florida Statutes (2013);

2. The defendant was attempting to collect a debt from the plaintiff arising from a transaction that was primarily for personal, family, or household purposes;

3. In seeking to collect the consumer debt from the plaintiff, the defendant knowingly and willfully used or threatened to use violence in violation of section 559.72(2), Florida Statute (2013);

4. As a result of the defendant's actions, the plaintiff has sustained damages.

A plaintiff preparing a statement of claim based upon this violation of the Florida Consumer Collection Practices Act should draft the statement of claim in such a way to ensure that the elements are clearly stated. As mentioned, in carefully drafting the statement of claim a plaintiff provides himself with a roadmap for the trial. He must prove every element at trial to recover a judgment.

An example of a statement of claim based upon this example of a violation of the Florida Consumer Collection Practices Act, which includes the elements described above and which will ultimately need to be proven at trial, is as follows:

STATEMENT OF CLAIM

Plaintiff, Carl Consumer, sues Defendant, Karla Kollector, and alleges:

Defendant is a person as defined by section 559.55, Florida Statutes (2013), and Defendant was attempting to collect a debt from Plaintiff arising from Plaintiff's purchase of a kitchen table and chairs, a transaction which was primarily for personal, family, or household purposes. In seeking to collect this consumer debt from Plaintiff, Defendant knowingly and willfully threatened to punch Plaintiff in the nose and to kick him in the shins in violation of section 559.72(2), Florida Statute (2013). As a result of Defendant's actions, Plaintiff has sustained damages.

WHEREFORE, Plaintiff demands judgment for damages against Defendant.

To state his claim for a violation of the Florida Consumer Collection Practices Act using the above-referenced Walton County Clerk of Court form, a plaintiff would not "check" any of the money or rent blanks. Instead, he would write his claim in the "Additional Information" portion of the form.

There are generally several books in a county's law library dedicated to identifying causes of action and their elements. Plaintiffs should also consider consulting with an attorney about causes of action and their elements.

Finalizing the Statement of Claim

In the majority of small claims cases, the statement of claim is the only writing in the court's file that is penned by a party. Stated another way, the plaintiff usually has the only opportunity to draft a document for the judge to read. Like all first impressions, the potential value of this communication to a plaintiff's case cannot be overstated.

Plaintiffs who adhere to the best practices described above and take the time to carefully and properly identify the parties in the case and to fully express the elements of causes of action will not only communicate the substance of their claims, but also will implicitly communicate that they are prepared and care about their claims. Again, it is worth the extra effort and thorough attention. Even if a judge never reads it, plaintiffs who spend the time to properly prepare their statement of claim are better prepared for mediation and, if necessary, trial.

8

REQUESTING A JURY TRIAL

Generally speaking, parties in a small claims case have a constitutional right to a jury trial. Although some causes of action do not permit jury trials, most claims that find their way to Florida's small claims courts permit trial by jury.

In a jury trial, a panel of six people decides the case. In a non-jury trial — generally referred to as a "*bench trial*" — a judge decides the case. Almost all small claims trials are bench trials.[30]

If a plaintiff wants a jury trial, he needs to ask for a jury when he files the statement of claim.[31]

It is important to note that the statement of claim forms provided by Florida's clerks of court do not contain a prompt for requesting a jury trial. Thus, a plaintiff who is seeking a jury trial and using a clerk-provided form should state at the end of the explanation of his claim, "Plaintiff demands a jury trial." A plaintiff creating his own statement of claim should likewise state such a demand therein.

If a plaintiff does not include a jury trial demand in his statement of claim, he may file a separate "*demand for jury trial*" at the same time as he files the statement of claim. However, the best practice is to include the demand for a jury trial within the statement of claim because it

---

[30] During fiscal year 2006-2007, 210,308 small claims cases were filed in Florida: only 82, or .03% of all of the cases, were resolved via jury trials. The Florida Senate, Committee on Judiciary, "Review of the Small Claims Process in Florida." Interim Report 2009-121, at 4 (Oct. 2008), *available* at http://archive.flsenate.gov/data/Publications/2009/Senate/reports/interim_reports/pdf/2009-121ju.pdf.

[31] Fla. Sm. Cl. R. 7.150.

eliminates extra (unnecessary) paperwork while ensuring that the other parties and judge are aware of the jury trial demand.

A defendant who wants a jury trial needs to ask for a jury, in writing, within five days of being served with the notice to appear or at the pretrial conference.[32] (A defendant's demand for jury trial form is included within the appendix of this book.)

If either party makes a timely request for a jury trial, then the right to have a jury decide the case is preserved. If neither party makes a timely request for a jury trial, then the right to a jury trial is waived. In other words, if neither party makes a timely request a jury trial, the trial will be conducted by the judge via a bench trial.

The choice of a jury trial is more difficult than concluding that a group may make a more favorable decision than a single judge.

The decision to request a jury trial depends upon how hard a party wants to work or how much he wants to pay a lawyer to work. A jury trial is much more complicated than a bench trial. Jury trials are difficult to conduct and manage — even for lawyers. Many books have been written to help lawyers learn how to select a jury, what sorts of jurors one might want to hear certain cases, and how jurors might be excluded or included on a panel. Obtaining information from prospective jurors to establish the bases for challenges for cause and making peremptory challenges is, to say the least, difficult. Plus, jury instructions must be prepared in advance of the trial to explain to the jury the legal principles that apply to the case. There is a lot more work involved.

On the other hand, the fact that so many cases are resolved by bench trials as opposed to jury trials in all Florida's trial courts means that few lawyers are proficient with jury trials. A non-lawyer willing to put in some effort to become knowledgeable about trial procedures and evidentiary matters might find himself on similar footing with a lawyer in a jury trial. In addition, a judge in a small claims proceeding is obliged to assist any party not represented by an attorney on courtroom

---

[32] *Id.*

decorum and the order of presentation of material evidence.[33] Finally, a non-lawyer who is opposed by a lawyer might be more appealing to a jury.[34]

Nevertheless, the time, effort, and expense associated with a jury trial makes it unlikely that it ever makes sense to request a jury trial in a small claims case.[35]

---

[33] Fla. Sm. Cl. R. 7.135(e).

[34] A jury consultant observed a few years ago that "jurors seem to distrust lawyers more these days. They each come into the courtroom with an idea of the stereotypical dishonest lawyer seared into their brains, and for many jurors, you are guilty of being that stereotypical lawyer until proven innocent." Posting of Marc S. Hurd, http://thpersonalinjury.blogspot.com/2010/03/juror-perceptions-of-trial-lawyers.html (March 3, 2010, 8:28 EST).

[35] Unless you are Groucho Marx who once quipped, "I was married by a judge. I should have asked for a jury."

9

THE NOTICE TO APPEAR

After filing the statement of claim, the clerk's office will give the plaintiff a case number and notice of the date, time, and place for the *"pretrial conference."*[36]

The pretrial conference — sometimes called a preliminary hearing — is not the final hearing or trial. The purpose of the pretrial conference is to bring together the parties in an attempt to amicably resolve the dispute and, if that is not possible, to determine the issues in dispute. In other words, the pretrial conference is a meeting to determine whether the lawsuit will require a trial.

The clerk's office is required to schedule the pretrial conference not more than 50 days from the date the statement of claim is filed.[37]

The clerk's office will also prepare a summons called a *"Notice to Appear"* for each defendant. The notice to appear is intended to notify the defendant of the pretrial conference and to provide some additional information about how the now-pending small claims case will proceed and the defendant's rights. The notice to appear must be served on each defendant along with a copy of the statement of claim.[38]

Although there are slight differences among the notice to appear forms used by Florida's clerks, most appear as the following form used by the Miami-Dade Clerk's offices.

---

[36] Fla. Sm. Cl. R. 7.050(d) and 7.090(b).

[37] Fla. Sm. Cl. R. 7.090(b).

[38] Fla. Sm. Cl. R. 7.060(b).

KURT E. LEE, ESQ. & TIM W. SOBCZAK, ESQ.

IN THE COUNTY COURT IN AND FOR MIAMI-DADE COUNTY, FLORIDA.

DIVISION	NOTICE TO APPEAR FOR PRETRIAL CONFERENCE	CASE NUMBER
☐ CIVIL		
☐ OTHER	(File in Quadruplicate)	SP05 SECTION NO.

PLAINTIFF(S)	VS. DEFENDANT(S)	SERVICE
_____	_____	
_____	_____	
_____	_____	

DEFENDANT(S) TO BE SERVED AT:

_____

_____

_____

_____

CLOCK IN

STATE OF FLORIDA

NOTICE TO PLAINTIFF(S) AND DEFENDANT(S)

YOU ARE HEREBY NOTIFIED that you are required to appear in person or by attorney at:

73 West Flagler St., Miami, Florida, Sixth Floor, Courtroom 6-4 on _____, 20_____.

at _____ . M., for pretrial conference before a Judge of this Court. Section # _____.

IMPORTANT-READ CAREFULLY

THE CASE WILL NOT BE TRIED AT THAT TIME.

DO NOT BRING WITNESSES — APPEAR IN PERSON OR BY ATTORNEY

The defendant(s) must appear in court on the date specified in order to avoid a default judgment. The plaintiff(s) must appear to avoid having the case dismissed for lack of prosecution. A written MOTION or ANSWER to the court by the plaintiff(s) or the defendant(s) shall not excuse the personal appearance of a party or its attorney in the PRETRIAL CONFERENCE. The date and time of the pretrial conference CANNOT be rescheduled without good cause and prior court approval.

A corporation may be represented at any stage of the trial court proceedings by an officer of the corporation or any employee authorized in writing by an officer of the corporation. Written authorization must be brought to the Pretrial Conference.

The purpose of the pretrial conference is to record your appearance, to determine if you admit all or part of the claim, to enable the court to determine the nature of the case, and to set the case for trial if the case cannot be resolved at the pretrial conference. You or your attorney should be prepared to confer with the court and to explain briefly the nature of your dispute, state what efforts have been made to settle the dispute, exhibit any documents necessary to prove the case, state the names and addresses of your witnesses, stipulate to the facts that will require no proof and will expedite the trial, and estimate how long it will take to try the case.

IMPORTANT – SEE REVERSE

CLK/CT. 389 Rev. 02/11   Clerk's web address: www.miami-dadeclerk.com

Mediation may take place at the pretrial conference. Whoever appears for a party must have full authority to settle. Failure to have full authority to settle at this pretrial conference may result in the imposition of costs and attorney fees incurred by the opposing party.

If you admit the claim, but desire additional time to pay, you must come and state the circumstances to the court. The court may or may not approve a payment plan and withhold judgment or execution or levy.

RIGHT TO VENUE: The law gives the person or company who has sued you the right to file in any one of several places as listed below. However, if you have been sued in any place other than one of these places, you, as the defendant(s), have the right to request that the case be moved to a proper location or venue. A proper location or venue may be one of the following:

1. Where the contract was entered into.

2. If the suit is on an unsecured promissory note, where the note is signed or where the maker resides.

3. If the suit is to recover property or to foreclosure a lien, where the property is located.

4. Where the event giving rise to the suit occurred.

5. Where any one or more of the defendants sued reside.

6. Any location agreed to in a contract.

7. In any action for money due, if there is no agreement as to where suit may be filed, where payment is to be made.

If you, as the defendant(s), believe the plaintiff(s) has/have not sued in one of these correct places, you must appear on your court date and orally request a transfer, or you must file a WRITTEN request for transfer in affidavit form (sworn to under oath) with the court 7 days prior to your first court date and send a copy to the plaintiff(s) or plaintiff's(s') attorney, if any.

A copy of the statement of claim shall be served with this summons.

HARVEY RUVIN CLERK OF THE COURTS	BY:_____ DEPUTY CLERK	DATE
COPY TO ☐ Mailed ☐ Attorney	☐ Hand-Delivered ☐ Plaintiff ☐ Process Server ☐ Sheriff	COURT SEAL

FILED BY:
ADDRESS:
TELEPHONE:

AMERICANS WITH DISABILITIES ACT OF 1990
ADA NOTICE

If you are a person with a disability who needs any accommodation in order to participate in this proceeding, you are entitled, at no cost to you, to the provision of certain assistance. Please contact the Eleventh Judicial Circuit Court's ADA Coordinator, Lawson E. Thomas Courthouse Center, 175 NW 1st Ave., Suite 2702, Miami, FL 33128, Telephone (305) 349-7175; TDD (305) 349-7174, Fax (305) 349-7355 at least 7 days before your scheduled court appearance, or immediately upon receiving this notification if the time before the scheduled appearance is less than 7 days; if you are hearing or voice impaired, call 711.

IMPORTANT – SEE REVERSE

CLK/CT. 389 Rev. 02/11   Clerk's web address: www.miami-dadeclerk.com

10

SERVING THE NOTICE TO APPEAR AND STATEMENT OF CLAIM

Each person or business named as a defendant in the statement of claim must be "*served*" with "*process.*" Documents are "*served*" on a business or person when they are delivered in certain ways to the business or person. "*Process*" refers to the statement of claim and the notice to appear. A copy of both the statement of claim and the notice to appear must be delivered in a legally prescribed manner to each of the defendants before the case may proceed.[39]

There are several ways to serve the notice to appear and statement of claim upon a defendant in a Florida small claims case.

Certified Mail

Defendants who are individuals and Florida residents may be served by certified mail. A plaintiff can have the clerk or his attorney send the lawsuit papers to the defendant via certified mail with delivery verified by a return receipt signed by the defendant or someone authorized to receive mail at the residence or principal place of business of the defendant.[40] A plaintiff cannot have the clerk serve initial process via certified mail upon a corporation or an out-of-state defendant.

---

[39] Fla. Sm. Cl. R. 7.070.

[40] *Id.*; *But see Heritage Corp. of S. Florida v. Rivas*, 289 So. 2d 432, 434 (Fla. 3d DCA 1974) ("A small claims court cannot acquire in personam jurisdiction over a non-resident defendant by registered or certified mail ...").

Personal Service

All defendants — individuals who are Florida residents and those who are non-residents and businesses — can be personally served with process. The initial filings are personally delivered by a Sheriff's deputy or private process server:

> a. Directly to the defendant, or

> b. To someone over the age of 15 with whom the defendant lives.

A plaintiff cannot himself serve process upon a defendant by hand delivery. Personal service must be made by the Sheriff's department in the county where the defendant lives or works or by a private process server who is certified in the county where the defendant lives or works.[41]

In most Florida counties, there are private process servers who, for a fee, will personally serve the statement of claim and notice to appear upon a defendant.

Whether served by a Sheriff's office or private process server, there is a fee for such service to be paid by the plaintiff or the party requesting service of process. It is also the responsibility of the plaintiff or party requesting service of process to furnish the Sheriff or private process server with the notice to appear, signed and sealed by the clerk, along with sufficient copies of the statement of claim or paper being served so that the Sheriff or process server might provide a copy to each party.

The best practice for serving the notice to appear and statement of claim to both individuals and businesses is to employ a private process server. Although a private process server's services will cost a little more than the Sheriff's offices, private process servers will update the plaintiff of the server's efforts in trying to locate and serve defendants.

---

[41] St. Lucie County Clerk of Courts, Self Help Center, http://www.stlucieclerk.com/index.php/services/file-cases-petitions/self-service-center (last visited January 14, 2014).

And, like the Sheriff's department fee, a private process server's fee may be recovered from the defendants as a taxable cost if the plaintiff prevails at trial.

If a defendant cannot be served by certified mail or by personal service, then there may be other methods for serving the initial lawsuit papers upon a defendant. The availability of other methods of service, however, will be dependent upon the claims being made, the problems being encountered with efforts to serve the defendant, and possibly other factors. As a result, if neither of the two methods of service described here are viable, an attorney should be consulted.

11

THE PRETRIAL CONFERENCE

The first "event" in a small claims case is the pretrial conference. All parties are required to attend the pretrial conference: plaintiffs and defendants. Indeed, the "Notice to Appear" which is served upon the defendants in a small claims action is commanding them to appear at the pretrial conference. The pretrial conference is, essentially, a meeting between the parties to the lawsuit and the judge or his representative to ensure that the defendants have been properly served and brought before the court, to ensure that the county where the lawsuit was filed is a proper county for so doing, and to provide an opportunity for the parties to resolve the dispute on their own or, failing that, to schedule the trial date.

The county court judge assigned to particular small claims cases usually presides over the pretrial conferences. However, the pretrial conference may be managed by non-judicial personnel employed by, or under contract with the court.[42]

All parties or their respective attorneys must appear at the pretrial conference. Failure to do so may result in the dismissal of the claims being made by the absent party or the entry of a default judgment against the absent party.[43] If a plaintiff's statement of claim—or a

---

[42] Fla. Sm. Cl. R. 7.090(b).

[43] Fla. Sm. Cl. R. 7.090(a). A default judgment may be entered against a defendant who fails to appear at a small claims pre-trial conference even if the defendant files a motion to dismiss before the conference. *Palatka Auto Auction, Inc. v. First Nat. Bank of Merritt Island*, 191 So. 2d 450, 453 (Fla. 4th DCA 1966)("Under the circumstances herein it would be manifestly unjust to say that, if the defendant fails, without explanation, to appear at the hearing, the court cannot properly enter a default judgment.").

defendant's counterclaim—is dismissed, the affected party loses his filing fees and must start all over again if he wants to pursue his claims. If a defendant or a counterclaim defendant fails to appear and a default judgment is entered, then there will be no trial and the entered judgment will award plaintiff or counterclaim plaintiff the relief sought in the statement of claim or counterclaim.

Note: Defendants or their attorneys need to attend the pretrial conference even if a defensive motion or some other paper contesting the allegations in the statement of claim is filed. The filing of a motion or other paper will not excuse the personal appearance of a defendant or such defendant's attorney at the pretrial conference.[44]

The best practice is to plan on arriving at the designated courtroom at least 15 minutes before the pretrial conference. This advice is practical in nature because, in all likelihood, many small claims cases have been scheduled to come before the judge or his representative for a pretrial conference. By arriving a little early, parties or their attorneys might secure a seat in the courtroom, have time to ask for any necessary assistance from the courtroom deputy or clerk, ensure that all electronic devices are turned off, and be prepared to respond when the case is called.

At the appointed time, the deputy or clerk will call the courtroom to order and ask everyone to stand while the judge enters the courtroom. The judge will take his place in the courtroom and then explain his procedure for the pretrial conferences.

Generally speaking, the judge will observe that there is a value to the parties to reach a settlement agreement, if possible, as opposed to having the judge render a decision. For example, defendants who owe the money claimed by a plaintiff can, through a settlement agreement, come up with a payment plan. For another example, plaintiffs, recognizing that there is more value to a dollar today as opposed to a dollar tomorrow, might agree to accept a lesser amount than that which is due so that they might also avoid coming back to court for a

---

[44] *Palatka Auto Auction, Inc.*, 191 So. 2d at 453; Fla. Sm. Cl. R. 7.090(c).

trial and possibly losing at trial. The judge will state that, if the matter goes to trial, he can generally only rule in favor of one of the parties and the judgment will not contain a payment plan. The judge will also likely caution the parties that, at trial, they will not likely be provided additional time to call a missing witness or locate a missing document. The judge or his clerk will then start calling the cases and will ask the parties or their attorneys who are present to come forward and stand before the judge when their case is called.

After confirming that the proper people are present, the judge, hearing officer, or a clerk of court representative may ask the defendant if he admits or denies the debt alleged by the plaintiff.[45] It is customary to refer to the judge as "Your Honor" when speaking to the judge or responding to the judge's questions. If the defendant denies that he owes the debt to the plaintiff, disagrees with the amounts sought, or advises the court that he has a legal defense, then the parties will likely be offered the opportunity to "*mediate*" their case.[46]

While it's not "an offer you can't refuse," the best practice is to agree to mediation.

First, refusing to mediate will unnecessarily annoy the judge (i.e., the person who may ultimately be deciding the outcome of the case). None of the parties are required to settle their claims at mediation. Indeed, if a party is so inclined, he may simply leave the courtroom and tell the mediator that he does not want to settle his claim and thereby dispense with mediation without displeasing the judge.

Second, parties should go to mediation to hear what the other parties might later say at trial. Given the limited opportunities in a small claims case to gain information about the other side's position, mediation is an invaluable tool for preparing a case for trial.

Third, parties should go to mediation because they will probably end up settling the case. Most small claims cases are resolved at

---

[45] The Florida Bar, Small claims: The who, what, where and why of collection lawsuits, https://www.floridabar.org/tfb/TFBConsum.nsf/0a92a6dc28e76ae58525700a005d0d53/eeb823f77975d746852579ba006b9edd!OpenDocument (last visited January 14, 2014).
[46] *Id.*

mediation and do not require a trial. By resolving the dispute through mediation, the parties avoid the time and expense of a trial and the uncertainty associated with having a third party—the judge—decide who will be the winner. People who reach a mediated settlement are much more likely to perform as they promised than people who receive a judgment through trial.[47]

Mediation

It appears to be the practice in all of Florida's small claims courts to initially direct the parties to mediation.[48] This practice is no doubt encouraged by Florida Small Claims Rule 7.130(b) which states, in pertinent part, "[s]ettlements in full or by installment payments made by the parties out of the presence of the court are encouraged."

An attorney may appear on behalf of a party at mediation if the attorney has full authority to settle without further consultation.[49] Similarly and unless otherwise ordered by the court, a non-lawyer representative—such as a spouse, friend, office manager, or billing clerk—may appear on behalf of a party in a small claims mediation if the representative has the party's signed written authority to appear at mediation and has full authority to settle without further consultation.[50] If an unauthorized person appears for mediation, the court may impose a sanction against the non-compliant party in the form of the costs and attorney fees incurred by the opposing party.[51] The authorization form for corporations provides the authority for the non-attorney representative to appear at mediation. An example of a form authorizing a non-lawyer to represent a party other than a corporation at mediation is as follows:

---

[47] Small Claims Advisory Service, Before Small Claims Court, http://www.hcs.harvard.edu/~scas/wp/wordpress/?page_id=12 (last visited January 14, 2014).

[48] Fla. Sm. Cl. R. 7.090(f).

[49] Id.

[50] Id.

[51] Id.

(CAPTION)

AUTHORIZATION TO ATTEND MEDIATION

_____(name of representative) is authorized to represent me at the mediation of this action and has full authority to settle this action without further consultation with me.

Pursuant to §92.525, Florida Statutes, and under penalties of perjury, I declare that I have read the foregoing and the facts stated in it are true.

Dated: _____

_____
(signature)

Printed name _____

Address: _____

_____

Phone number: _____

The Mediator's Introduction

The mediation process begins with the mediator.[52] In many Florida counties, the mediators of small claims cases are retirees who have volunteered their time to help people resolve their small claims disputes; the mediator will not be the judge assigned to the small claims case.

Mediation begins with the mediator's introduction.[53] The mediator will explain the mediation process and the role of the mediator.[54] The mediator will explain that the parties make the decisions.[55] The mediator will not decide who is "right" or who is "wrong." The mediator will not enter an order or a judgment nor will the mediator report to the judge whom he thinks is "right" or whom he thinks should "win"

---

[52] Florida Supreme Court, Mediation in Florida, http://www.flcourts.org/gen_public/adr/MediationInformation/WhatExpectMediationGenPub.html (last visited January 14, 2014).

[53] *Id.*

[54] *Id.*

[55] *Id.*

the case. The mediator will explain that what is said during mediation is, generally speaking, confidential and that each party may prevent the other from telling the judge what was said or admitted during the mediation session.[56]

Although the mediator's introduction is likely a rehearsed statement, the best practice is to listen carefully. During the mediator's introduction and explanation of the mediation process, a party might learn whether the mediator has any legal training, has any background as a business owner, or may have any preconceptions about the parties or the case. Although mediators serve as neutrals and endeavor to reflect impartiality, mediators are human and the subsequent opening statement and communications with the mediator might be more effective if they are expressed in "mediator-friendly" terms.

For example, if the mediator is a retired CPA, a party might tailor his mediation presentation to focus upon the numbers and calculations involved in the case. If, for another example, the mediator is a social worker, a party might focus his presentation upon the interpersonal relationships involved in the dispute and how the other party angrily disrupted the office when he refused to pay his invoice.

Opening Statements by the Parties

The mediator's introduction and explanation of the mediation process is usually followed by an opportunity for the parties to explain their positions.[57] The mediator usually begins with the plaintiff and the plaintiff's opening statement before hearing from the defendant. The mediator may help the parties express themselves while keeping interruptions to a minimum.[58]

Generally speaking, a plaintiff's opening statement is a description of his claim and a defendant's opening statement is a description of the reasons why plaintiff's claim is ill-founded. A defendant with

---

[56] *Id.*

[57] *Id.*

[58] *Id.*

a counterclaim would, of course, describe such claim as part of his opening statement.

The most effective opening statements are those given by parties who appear calm and polite. Lawsuits are stressful and mediation is the first opportunity the parties will have to talk to someone in a courthouse about their respective cases in the presence of the other party. Given the situation, a party might feel that it is important to convince the mediator that his position is the correct one and that the opposing party is wrong. A party might also feel angry or upset with the other. These feelings are understandable but they will, however, get in the way of an effective presentation at mediation and, later if necessary, at trial. The mediator is not going to make any decision in the action; he is only interested in having the parties enter into an agreement that will dispense with the necessity of a trial. Parties that are angry or impolite are generally less persuasive than parties who appear to be calm and civil. So, stay calm and polite.

Effective opening statements also usually involve the parties disclosing and discussing key information, documents, and things. Deciding on what is important at mediation is somewhat different than what might be important at trial because the parties are trying to persuade each other at mediation whereas at trial the parties are attempting to persuade a neutral third party. The decision about what to disclose at mediation should also be guided by the realization that an agreement might not be reached at mediation and the action may need to proceed to trial.

It is important to listen carefully to the other party's opening statement and other communications. One can gather important information about the other's contentions and legal positions, which might be useful at trial if the matter does not settle at mediation. For example, if the other party is arguing at mediation that the asserted claims are untimely and are barred by a statute of limitations, the listener will want to ensure that he is prepared at trial to demonstrate that the claims are not time barred. Conversely and because each party should assume the other is paying careful attention at mediation, mediation participants should not disclose anything they do not want the other party to know.[59]

Caucuses and Mediated Agreements

After these initial procedures and opening statements, the mediation process varies.[60] The mediator may continue to meet with the parties together to discuss the situation in an effort to help the parties come to a resolution.[61] The mediator might also separate the parties and, then, meet or "*caucus*" with each party individually in an effort to find out how the dispute might be resolved.[62] For example, if the defendant appears at the pretrial conference and admits he owes the plaintiff money but needs time to pay, the mediator may meet with the plaintiff separately to determine whether and what sort of payment plan might be acceptable and then meet separately with the defendant to find out his capacity to comply with an acceptable payment plan.

No one can be forced to remain at mediation. But, mediators will encourage all of the parties to give mediation a chance to succeed.[63]

If a total or partial agreement is reached, the agreement will be written and the parties will sign the agreement.[64] Mediation agreements are sometimes referred to as "*stipulations*." A mediation agreement will be binding and enforceable upon the parties like any other contract. In

---

[59] Communications made within a mediation may be confidential, but one cannot erase the other party's memory. Although the other party cannot later testify that you said something at mediation, the other party can use information gleaned at mediation to identify documents, witnesses, and other evidence for use at trial.

[60] Florida Supreme Court, Mediation in Florida, http://www.flcourts.org/gen_public/adr/MediationInformation/WhatExpectMediationGenPub.html (last visited January 14, 2014).

[61] *Id.*

[62] *Id.*

[63] *Id.*

[64] *Id.*; Fla. Sm. Cl. R. 7.090(g).

addition, the judge overseeing the small claims case has the authority to enter the agreement as an order of the court.[65]

In the case of stipulations involving performance by a party after the mediation—e.g., payment plans, surrender of rental property on a specified date, return of stolen property—judges often include the mediation agreement as part of an order for conditional stay. This sort of order allows the small claims case to remain pending while the parties comply with the terms and conditions of the mediation agreement. If the parties fully comply with the mediation agreement, the case is dismissed. If, however, a party does not comply with the agreement, the other may submit an affidavit to the judge describing the other party's non-compliance and a judgment, if appropriate, will be entered against the non-compliant party without another hearing.

---

[65] *Id.*

Mediator's Introduction

Plaintiff's Opening Statement

Defendant's Opening Statement

Mediator Caucuses with the Parties

Parties Sign a Written Agreement

Progress of a Successful Mediation

If No Agreement is Reached at Mediation

If no agreement is reached at mediation, the parties will return to the courtroom so that the court might complete the pretrial conference and schedule the matter for trial.

The mediator will only advise the judge that the mediation reached an "*impasse*." The mediator will not tell the judge that one party or the other was unreasonable, anything that was said at mediation, nor who he thinks should win the case.

To complete the pretrial conference, the court or presiding officer will discuss the following matters with the parties:[66]

> 1. A simplification of the issues. For example, a defendant in a case seeking payment of money might be asked why he does not believe he owes the money so that the trial might focus on this defense as opposed to some other issue about which there is no real dispute.

> 2. The necessity or desirability of amendments to the statement of claim.

> 3. The possibility of obtaining admissions of fact and documents that avoid unnecessary proof at trial. Are there some facts to which the parties agree? Are there some documents that the parties agree should be admitted into evidence? The notice to appear specifically provides that parties should be prepared to exhibit at the pretrial conference any documents necessary to prove the case.[67]

> 4. Limitations on the number of witnesses. How many people will the plaintiff and defendant call as witnesses? Are there witnesses who are not necessary because their

---

[66] Fla. Sm. Cl. R. 7.090(b).

[67] 41 Fla. Jur 2d Pre-Trial Proceedings § 18.

anticipated testimony will be needlessly repetitious? The notice to appear specifically provides that parties need to be prepared at the pretrial conference to state the names and addresses of the party's witnesses.[68]

5. The possibilities of settlement. Mediation may have been unsuccessful, but perhaps an agreement can be reached if a party verifies a fact or provides some additional information to the other.

6. Any other matters as the court in its discretion deems necessary. This "catch all" category may include anything from the coordination of the parties' and court's schedules to the summary disposition of the case. Generally speaking, courts have more cases to process than they do time. Therefore, courts generally focus upon items 1 through 5 and they do so relatively quickly.

---

[68] *Id.*

12

FAILURE TO APPEAR AT THE PRETRIAL CONFERENCE

If a party is unable to appear at the pretrial conference or needs additional time to investigate the matter or prepare a response to the statement of claim, he should contact the other parties and attempt to reschedule the conference.[69] If the other parties agree to reschedule, then the parties must notify the clerk in writing. The party requesting the new pretrial conference should then follow-up with the clerk's office to verify that that the pretrial conference was, in fact, canceled or rescheduled.

If the other parties do not agree to reschedule, then the party needing to reset the pretrial conference may ask the court for a *"continuance."* The party seeking a continuance must file a written motion before the pretrial conference or he may make an oral motion at the pretrial conference.[70] Motions are discussed in greater detail later in this book, but a motion for continuance is a request to the court asking that the pretrial conference be rescheduled for a later date. The party seeking a continuance will need to show *"good cause"* to justify the continuance and, thus, one drafting such a motion should include all of the reasons why the party is requesting that the pretrial conference be rescheduled and should note when the rescheduled

---

[69] *See e.g.,* Volusia County Clerk of Court, Small Claims, http://www.clerk.org/html/small-claims.html (last visited January 14, 2014).

[70] *See* Fla. Sm. Cl. R. 7.130(a).

pretrial conference should occur.[71] A copy of the written motion needs to be provided to all of the other parties to the small claims case.[72]

Merely filing a motion requesting a new pretrial conference date does not guarantee that a continuance will be granted.[73] A party seeking a continuance on the basis of his inability to attend the pretrial conference should monitor the case to learn whether the court granted the motion and when his appearance will be required.[74]

A party should never, under any circumstance, simply no-show for the pretrial conference (or any other court event) because the case may proceed without the party's attendance.[75] Indeed, if some emergency arises that prevents a party from attending the pretrial conference or any other court event the affected party should call the judge's judicial assistant and alert the assistant to the emergency.[76]

If a plaintiff simply fails to appear at the pretrial conference without making any contact with the clerk, the court will likely dismiss the case.[77]

If a defendant fails to appear at the pretrial conference without making any contact with the clerk, the court may—after verifying that the case was filed in the proper county and that the defendant was legally notified—enter a default judgment against him without further notice or hearing.[78]

---

[71] Fla. Sm. Cl. R. 7.130(a); *cf. Stern v. Four Freedoms Nat. Med. Services, Co.*, 417 So. 2d 1085, 1086 (Fla. 3d DCA 1982)(upholding denial of motion for continuance of trial where plaintiff failed to indicate when she would be available).

[72] Fla. Sm. Cl. R. 7.080.

[73] Volusia County Clerk of Court, *supra* note 72.

[74] Volusia County Clerk of Court, *supra* note 72.

[75] Volusia County Clerk of Court, *supra* note 72.

[76] *See* Volusia County Clerk of Court, *supra* note 72.

[77] Fla. Sm. Cl. R. 7.160(a).

[78] Volusia County Clerk of Court, *supra* note 72.

13

DEMANDS FOR JUDGMENT/ OFFERS OF JUDGMENT/OFFERS OF SETTLEMENT

Section 768.79, Florida Statutes, provides a procedure for plaintiffs and defendants to make formalized settlement proposals. This statutory procedure is sometimes referred to as making "*demands for judgment,*" "*offers of judgment,*" or "*offers of settlement.*" If a recipient of a settlement proposal made pursuant to section 768.79 does not accept it, he might be later obligated to pay the offeror's attorneys' fees.[79]

Because this statutory provision involves the recovery of attorneys' fees and would, presumably, only be invoked by a party who is represented by an attorney, a discussion of this provision is beyond the scope of this book.[80] However, if a party who is not represented by an attorney receives a demand for judgment, offer of judgment, offer of settlement, or other document which makes reference to section 768.79, he should immediately consult with his own attorney because

---

[79] *State Farm Mut. Automobile Ins. Co. v. Nichols,* 932 So. 2d 1067 (Fla.2006)(applying section 768.79, Florida Statutes, to small claims).

[80] An example of a complicated case involving this statutory provision is *Bristol W. Ins. Co. v. Care Therapy & Diagnostics, Inc.,* 05-11365, 2008 WL 4005713 (Fla. 13th Cir. Ct. 2008).

there is a 30 day time limit to accept such a settlement offer or it is deemed to have been rejected.[81]

---

[81] An overview of the statute's procedures and a sense of the statute's complexity in application may be found in this Hillsborough County Bar Association publication: Hillsborough County Bar Association, https://www.hillsbar.com/UserFiles/Offers%20 of%20Judgment.pdf (last visted January 10, 2014).

14

DEFENDING AGAINST THE
STATEMENT OF CLAIM

Unless required by order of court, written pretrial motions and defensive pleadings are not necessary.[82] Unlike all other civil lawsuits in Florida, defendants in small claims cases do not need to file a written "*answer*" to the plaintiff's claims nor do they need to file written "*affirmative defenses*" to such claims. All a defendant must do is appear, in person or through his attorney, at the time specified in the notice to appear.[83]

Note: The absence of written responses to a statement of claim does not mean, however, that a defendant does not have the ability to defend himself in a Florida small claims court proceeding. A small claims defendant has the same rights and defenses as a defendant in a case seeking damages in excess of $5,000.

A defendant's primary defense against a claim is to disprove a plaintiff's allegation or to demonstrate that a plaintiff has failed to prove a key portion of his claim. A defendant should research the claims made against him to determine which elements will need to be proven by the plaintiff. As stated earlier in conjunction with what a plaintiff should include in his statement of claim, there are generally several books in a county's law library dedicated to identifying causes of action and their elements. Plaintiffs need to prove all of the elements to prevail on their claim; defendants need to disprove an element or

---

[82] Fla. Sm. Cl. R. 7.090(c).

[83] Henry P. Trawick, Florida Practice and Procedure § 11:9 (2013-2014 ed.).

bring to the judge's attention that plaintiff failed to prove an element to prevail in defense.

A secondary defense to a plaintiff's claim can be legal defenses or what are sometimes called "affirmative defenses." Affirmative defenses essentially say in response to a plaintiff's claim, "Yes, but," and almost every cause of action or claim has potential affirmative defenses that might be asserted. For example, if a plaintiff claims that a defendant promised to deliver five pairs of red shoes, an affirmative defense might be, "Yes, but the plaintiff knowingly and voluntarily waived his right to receive the red shoes when he agreed to accept $50 and four pairs of blue shoes." Potential affirmative defenses are often discussed in the same books that address causes of action in the county law library. Whereas plaintiffs have the "*burden*" to prove all of the elements of their claims against defendants, defendants have the burden of proving affirmative defenses and these defenses have elements of their own.

Defendants should consider consulting with an attorney about the elements of causes of action and affirmative defenses which pertain to their case.

Improper Venue Must be Asserted Before or at the Pretrial Conference

If a defendant in a small claims case has been sued in any place other than one of the places described in the notice to appear as a proper venue, he has the right to request that the case be dismissed or moved to a proper location or venue. The defendant either must appear at the pretrial conference and orally request a transfer or must file a written request for transfer in affidavit form (i.e., sworn to under oath) with the court seven days prior to the pretrial conference and send a copy to the plaintiff or plaintiff's attorney, if any.[84]

Counterclaims

Technically speaking, counterclaims are not defenses. Practically speaking however, counterclaims are defenses because, if successful, they can reduce or eliminate any debt or obligation a defendant owes to a plaintiff.

---

[84] Fla. Sm. Cl. R. 7.060(a).

For example, if Painting By Joe, Inc., sues Harry Homeowner for failing to pay $500 for painting Mr. Homeowner's garage floor, Mr. Homeowner might state as a counterclaim that he did not pay the contractor because the work was improperly done and because he had to pay another contractor to fix it. In a situation such as this, Mr. Homeowner must file a counterclaim that asks Painting By Joe, Inc., to pay him for the additional expenses in fixing the botched paint job. Mr. Homeowner can be reimbursed even if the amount he is asking for is more than what he owes Painting By Joe, Inc.

Although a defendant's defenses do not need to be in writing, counterclaims and allegations of set-offs must be filed with the clerk and be in writing.[85] Any claim the defendant has against the plaintiff arising out of the same transaction or occurrence that is the subject matter of the plaintiff's claim, known as a "*compulsory counterclaim*", must be filed at least five days before the pretrial conference or within such time as the court designates or it is deemed to be abandoned.[86] Any claim the defendant has against the plaintiff *not* arising out of the same transaction or occurrence that is the subject matter of the plaintiff's claim, known as a "*permissive counterclaim*," must also be filed at least five days before the pretrial conference or within such time as the court designates.[87] But, because it is not related to the transaction at issue in the plaintiff's claim, the permissive counterclaim is not abandoned if not pursued in the case. If a defendant needs additional time to prepare a defense or counterclaim, the defendant may ask the court to continue the pretrial conference.[88]

---

[85] Fla. Sm. Cl. R. 7.100(c).

[86] Fla. Sm. Cl. R. 7.100(a).

[87] Fla. Sm. Cl. R. 7.100(b). Counterclaims which do not arise out of the transaction or occurrence which is the subject matter of the plaintiff's claim are called "permissive counterclaims." Permissive counterclaims are not waived or abandoned if not timely asserted in a small claims case. A defendant having a permissive counterclaim might file a subsequent action against the plaintiff based upon such claims.

[88] Fla. Sm. Cl. R. 7.100(c).

When a defendant's counterclaim or set-off exceeds $5,000, the defendant still needs to file the written counterclaim or set-off with the clerk. The action will then be transferred to the court having jurisdiction over the matter.[89] For example, if a defendant asserts a counterclaim seeking $10,000 in damages from the plaintiff, then the case will be moved from the small claims division of the county court to the county court's regular civil division. In such an event, the counterclaimant must, as evidence of good faith, deposit the filing fee required by the court to which the case is to be transferred at the time the counterclaim is filed. A counterclaimant's failure to make the deposit waives the right to transfer. Defendants having counterclaims that exceed $5,000 should consult with a lawyer for assistance preparing the claim and causing it to be properly filed.

Contents of Counterclaim

A counterclaim is like a statement of claim for defendants. Defendants having counterclaims should write their claims as if they were the party initiating the small claims case. Thus, as explained earlier in the section entitled *The Statement of Claim*, the counterclaim should be drafted in such a manner that the proper counterclaim-defendants are properly named,[90] necessary written documents are attached to the counterclaim, and legal claims are asserted.

Defendants can use a statement of claim form and simply note in the title of the document that it is a counterclaim. Or, some clerk's

---

[89] Fla. Sm. Cl. R. 7.100(d).

[90] If a defendant has counterclaims against the plaintiff and others, then those "others" might also be joined to the action as counterclaim defendants. For example, if Mr. Homeowner has a counterclaim against Painting By Joe, Inc., based upon damage caused to his car when the painting company and a neighbor had a fist fight in his garage, Mr. Homeowner might file a counterclaim against both the plaintiff, Painting By Joe, Inc., and his neighbor. In such an instance, the "new" counterclaim defendant will need to be served with a notice to appear and the counterclaim. Defendants having counterclaims against others than the plaintiff should refer to the preceding section in this book entitled *Serving the Notice to Appear and Statement Of Claim* for directions regarding proper service of process.

offices, like those in Citrus County, have counterclaim forms available (which are simply statement of claims forms with the title changed to "counterclaim" and the names of the parties reversed in the introductory paragraph).

KURT E. LEE, ESQ. & TIM W. SOBCZAK, ESQ.

IN THE COUNTY COURT IN AND FOR CITRUS COUNTY
FIFTH JUDICIAL CIRCUIT OF FLORIDA

CASE NO:

Plaintiff(s)

-vs-

_____ Defendant(s)

COUNTERCLAIM

Comes now the Defendant(s) and files this his/her/their Counterclaim or Setoff to Plaintiff(s)'s Statement of Claim and alleges:

1. This is an action for damages which do not exceed the amount of $5,000.00 exclusive of costs, interest and attorneys' fees.
2. Said Defendant/Counterplaintiff(s) claims the amount of $_____ as being due from said Plaintiff/Counterdefendant(s) and alleges as the basis of said Counterclaim:

WHEREFORE Defendant/Counterplaintiff(s) demands judgment for damages against Plaintiff/Counterdefendant(s) in the sum of $_____ as Setoff to Plaintiff(s)'s Statement of Claim.

STATE OF FLORIDA
COUNTY OF CITRUS

The undersigned, being first duly sworn under oath, states the foregoing is just and true statement of the amount owing by the above named Plaintiff/Counterdefendant(s) to said Defendant/Counterplaintiff(s).

_____
AFFIANT

Subscribed and sworn to before me this ____ day of _____, A.D. 20 ___.

ANGELA VICK
CLERK OF THE COURT

By:_____
Deputy Clerk

Or:_____
Notary Public

C:\COUNTY\FORMS\SMALL CLAIMS\Counter clean/1/2003

-- 62 --

Failure to Timely File a Counterclaim

If a party has failed to timely file a counterclaim, i.e., it was not filed at least 5 days prior to the pretrial conference, the party should:

1. Immediately prepare the counterclaim.

2. Immediately prepare a motion asking the court to accept the untimely counterclaim and/or to continue the trial until such time as the defendant might be permitted to file the counterclaim.[91] A defendant will need to show "*good cause*" in the motion for the untimely filing, i.e., a defendant will need to explain to the court why his failure to timely file the counterclaim should be excused.

3. If the judge denies the motion and declines to accept the counterclaim, a defendant should still try to present his claims at the trial. In *Metro Ford, Inc. v. Green*, 724 So. 2d 706, 707 (Fla. 3d DCA 1999), a Florida District Court of Appeal ruled that a small claims court judge made a mistake by only deciding the claim set forth in the statement of claim rather than resolving the underlying dispute. In the *Metro Ford, Inc.* case, a plaintiff claimed that a car repair business had wrongfully taken his car when he refused to pay certain repair costs. The car repair business failed to make a written counterclaim for the unpaid repair costs. At trial, the small claims judge ruled against the plaintiff and expressed that she wanted to award the business the repair costs but determined, erroneously in the appellate court's opinion, that she could not do so in the absence of a written counterclaim. The appellate court found that the trial judge should have ruled on the entire dispute.

---

[91] *See* the section below entitled *Motions* for more details on the form and procedure.

Third-Party Complaints

Technically speaking, third-party complaints are not defenses. Practically speaking however, third-party complaints are defenses because, like counterclaims, if they are successful they can reduce or eliminate any debt or obligation a defendant owes to a plaintiff by having another party satisfy all or part of the debt or obligation.

For example and continuing the hypothetical situation set forth above, if Painting By Joe, Inc., sues Harry Homeowner for failing to pay $500 for painting Mr. Homeowner's garage floor, Mr. Homeowner might state as a third-party complaint that he did not pay the contractor because the developer that sold him the home, Residential Home Developer, LLC, was supposed to pay the contractor. In a situation such as this, Mr. Homeowner must file a third-party complaint against Residential Home Developer, LLC, that asks the developer to pay the claim made by Painting By Joe, Inc.

To bring a third-party defendant into a small claims case, a defendant may cause the statement of claim to be served on a person not a party to the case who is or may be liable to the defendant for all or part of the plaintiff's claim.[92] However, the best practice (and one which will help ensure that those who, instead of or in addition to defendant, are liable to plaintiff) is to file and serve a third-party complaint because such document will name the third-party defendants.

---

[92] Fla. Sm. Cl. R. 7.100(e).

Plaintiff/
Statement of Claim

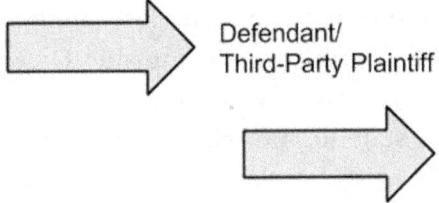

Defendant/
Third-Party Plaintiff

Third-Party Defendants/
Individuals or Entities
Defendant alleges are
responsible for Plaintiff's claims

A defendant wanting to file a third party complaint must obtain the court's permission to do so at the pretrial conference, and he must file the third-party complaint within such time as the court allows.[93]

Contents of Third-Party Complaints

A third-party complaint is like a statement of claim. Defendants having third-party claims should write their claims as if they were the party that was initiating the small claims case. Thus, as explained earlier in *The Statement of Claim* section, the third-party complaint should be drafted in such a manner that the proper third-party defendants are properly named, necessary written documents are attached to the third-party complaint, and legal claims are asserted. The original statement of claim (or counterclaim, as explained later) that roped in the third party should always be attached to a third-party complaint.

A defendant can use a statement of claim form and simply note in the title of the document that it is a third-party complaint. Or, some clerk's offices, like those in Pasco County, have third-party complaint forms available (which are simply statement of claims forms with the title changed to "third-party statement of claim" and the name of the defendant replacing that of the plaintiff and with the defendants designated as third-party defendants).

---

[93] *Id.*

DEFENDING AGAINST THE STATEMENT OF CLAIM

IN THE COUNTY COURT OF THE SIXTH JUDICIAL CIRCUIT
IN AND FOR PASCO COUNTY, FLORIDA

SMALL CLAIMS

_____

Case #: _____
Section: _____

_____

Third-Party Plaintiff(s)/Defendant(s)

VS.

_____
_____

Third-Party Defendant(s)

THIRD-PARTY STATEMENT OF CLAIM

Third-party Plaintiff(s) _____

sues third-party defendant(s) _____

and alleges: There is now due, owing and unpaid from the third-party defendant(s) to third-party plaintiff(s)

$_____ with interest since _____ for the following reason, to wit:

_____

_____

_____

_____

_____

_____

WHEREFORE, third-party plaintiff(s) demands judgment in the amount of $_____

for damages interest and all costs of this claim against third-party defendant(s).

I HAVE READ THE RIGHT TO VENUE STATEMENT ON THE NOTICE TO APPEAR AND I BELIEVE VENUE LIES
IN PASCO COUNTY.

DATE: _____

Third-party plaintiff
Phone # _____

Sworn and subscribed to before me this ____ day of _____

Paula S. O'Neil
Clerk & Comptroller
Pasco County, Florida

_____

Deputy Clerk

SMCL STATEMENT 3rd PARTY R01 0602

–– 67 ––

Although most third-party complaints are initiated by defendants, when a counterclaim is asserted against a plaintiff, the plaintiff may bring in third-party defendants under circumstances that would entitle a defendant to do so.[94] For example and again using the hypothetical situation set forth above, if defendant Harry Homeowner filed a counterclaim against Painting By Joe, Inc., alleging that he had to hire another contractor to repair Painting By Joe, Inc.'s defective garage painting; Painting By Joe, Inc., might file a third-party complaint against the paint manufacturer which supplied the defective paint asking that the paint manufacturer reimburse Mr. Homeowner for his repair costs and damages which are described in the counterclaim.

After a Third-Party Complaint is Permitted

If a third-party complaint is permitted, the clerk must schedule a supplemental pretrial conference and prepare a notice to appear for each third-party defendant.[95] The notices to appear must be served upon the third-party defendants with copies of the third-party complaint. Defendants having third-party claims should refer to the preceding section in this book entitled *Serving the Notice to Appear and Statement of Claim* for directions regarding proper service of process.

The procedure at the supplemental pretrial conference is similar to that of the initial pretrial conference. The defendant, now sometimes referred to as the third-party plaintiff, and the third-party defendants, must attend the supplemental pretrial conference personally or by their counsel.[96] If additional time is needed for a third-party defendant to prepare a defense, the court may continue the action.[97] The process of the supplemental pretrial conference is similar to that of the initial pretrial conference and third-party plaintiffs and defendants should refer to the preceding section in this book entitled *The Pretrial Conference.*

---

[94] *Id.*

[95] *Id.*

[96] *Id.*

[97] *Id.*

Third-Party Complaint May be Handled Separately by the Court

As demonstrated above, third-party claims, whether asserted by plaintiffs or defendants, cause the small claims action to be more time consuming and complex. Thus, the Florida Small Claims Rules permit any party—a plaintiff, defendant, or third-party defendant—to serve a motion asking the court to strike a third-party claim or to "*sever*" it from the main proceeding for a separate trial.[98]

Whether it would be worthwhile to seek separate handling of third-party claims probably depends upon the party's position in the small claims case, i.e., whether a party is seeking relief or is defending against claims for relief. In a situation where a defendant has filed a third-party complaint, a plaintiff should consider asking the court to sever or separate that complaint for separate handling and trial. A plaintiff in this circumstance wants to focus attention on his claims and his recovery and wants the judge or jury to neither be distracted by the defendant's claims nor be convinced that the defendant is somehow a "victim" who has been caught in the middle.

On the other hand, a defendant and third-party defendant in this circumstance might want to resist any effort to sever the third-party complaint for a separate trial: the defendant because he wants the third-party defendant to be primarily responsible for the defense against plaintiff's claims, and the third-party defendant because he wants to ensure that plaintiff's claims are defended and that the defendant does not accede to a judgment for which the third-party defendant might ultimately be responsible.

In a situation where a defendant has made a counterclaim and the plaintiff has made third-party claims, a similar analysis would probably apply. In this latter situation however, the defendant will likely want to sever the third-party claims and the plaintiff and third-party defendant will likely resist this effort.

---

[98] *Id.*

15

MOTIONS

A "*motion*" is any written or oral request for the court to make a particular ruling or order. The party filing the motion is sometimes referred to as the "*movant*."

Motions may be made before, during, or after trial, and may be made by any party in the case. Written motions should, at a minimum, include the case caption, identify the party or parties making the request, expressly state what relief or action is sought in the court order, and state the basis for the requested relief. Motions also need to include a certificate of service as explained in greater detail below.

Some of the most common types of motions in a small claims case are set forth below. Unless otherwise indicated, the listed motions do not have a stated deadline but should be made as soon as it is determined to be necessary.

> 1. **Motion to Amend** - A motion to amend asks the court for permission to allow an amendment of a statement of claim, counterclaim, or third-party complaint. The amended statement of claim, counterclaim, or third-party complaint that the movant seeks to file should be attached as an exhibit to the motion.
>
> 2. **Motion for Continuance** - A motion for continuance asks the court to delay the pretrial conference or trial. Motions

for continuance must show "*good cause*" for the requested delay.

3. **Motion to Accept Untimely Counterclaim** - A motion to accept an untimely counterclaim asks the court for permission to file a counterclaim after the deadline, which is five days prior to the pretrial conference date.

4. **Motion to File Third-Party Complaint** - A motion to file third-party complaint asks the court for permission to file a third-party complaint. This motion may be made orally at the pretrial conference, i.e., a party may ask the judge for permission to file a third party complaint at the pretrial conference. If a party is requesting permission to file a third-party complaint after the pretrial conference, then the motion should ask that the court accept the untimely third-party complaint.

5. **Motion to Strike** - A motion to strike asks the court to strike or remove from the case another party's claim or third-party claim.[99]

6. **Motion to Sever Third-Party Complaint** - A motion to sever asks the court to separate the proceedings on a third-party complaint from the proceedings on the original statement of claim.

7. **Motion to Dismiss for Failure to Prosecute** - A motion to dismiss for failure to prosecute asks the court to dismiss the small claims case because the plaintiff has failed to take any action in the case for a period of six months.[100]

---

[99] *Id.*

[100] Fla. Sm. Cl. R. 7.110(e).

8. **Motion for Costs** - A motion for costs is a post-trial
motion which asks the court to award the prevailing or
winning party the costs he incurred during the small claims
case.[101] A motion for costs must be served no later than 30
days after filing of the judgment, including a judgment of
dismissal, or the service of a notice of voluntary dismissal.[102]

9. **Motion for New Trial** - A motion for new trial is another
post-trial motion. A motion for new trial asks the court to
conduct a new trial based upon some error in the original
trial, such as an erroneous ruling on evidence.[103] A motion
for new trial must be filed no later than 10 days after the
return of a verdict in a jury action or the date of filing of
the judgment in a nonjury action. [104]

10. **Motion for Relief From Judgment or Order** - A motion
for relief from judgment or order asks the court to relieve
a party from the effects of an order or judgment based
upon a clerical mistake, inadvertence, surprise, excusable
neglect, newly discovered evidence, fraud, or because the
judgment is void or has been satisfied or released.[105] If a
motion for relief from judgment or order is based upon
mistake, inadvertence, surprise, excusable neglect, newly
discovered evidence, or fraud, the motion must be served
not later than one year after the judgment or order was
signed.[106]

---

[101] Fla. Sm. Cl. R. 7.175.
[102] *Id.*
[103] Fla. Sm. Cl. R. 7.180.
[104] *Id.*
[105] Fla. Sm. Cl. R. 7.190.
[106] *Id.*

11. **Motion for Hearing in Aid of Execution** - A motion for hearing in aid of execution is a post-trial motion. The movant is the party in whose favor the judgment was entered, and the movant asks the court to order the judgment debtor to appear at a hearing and testify about his earnings, financial status, and assets — sources that might be tapped to pay the judgment entered against him.[107]

12. **Motion for Issuance of Writ of Garnishment** - A motion for issuance of writ of garnishment is a post-trial motion asking the court to direct the clerk to issue a writ of garnishment.[108] A writ of garnishment is a legal document that directs someone who owes money to the judgment debtor to, instead, pay such money to the judgment creditor.

Most clerks' offices do not have a form for every type of motion. Indeed, many clerks do not provide any motion forms. An example of Motion for Relief from Judgment or Order provided by the Hillsborough County Clerk of Court follows and its general format, as opposed to its content, might be adopted for use in making other written requests of the court. Other form motions appear in the appendix.

---

[107] Fla. Sm. Cl. R. 7.221.

[108] *See* the *Collecting on Judgments* section below for more details.

**IN THE COUNTY COURT IN AND FOR HILLSBOROUGH COUNTY, FLORIDA
CIVIL DIVISION**

_____	*	CASE NO._____
_____	*	DIVISION_____
Plaintiff(s)		
		FLORIDA BAR NO. _____
vs.	*	
_____	*	
_____	*	
Defendant(s)		

MOTION FOR RELIEF FROM JUDGMENT OR ORDER

The Plaintiff_____/Defendant _____ moves to vacate, amend, or correct the _____, entered on _____, in this action for the following reasons:

1. ____   Clerical mistake.
2. ____   Mistake, inadvertence, surprise or excusable neglect.
3. ____   Newly discovered evidence not discoverable within ten (10) days after trial.
4. ____   Fraud, misrepresentation, or misconduct.
5. ____   Judgment is void or satisfied, released, or discharged.

EXPLANATION:_____

_____

Meritorious Defense (for setting aside default or judgment)

_____

_____

UNDER PENALTY OF PERJURY, I SWEAR OR AFFIRM THAT I BELIEVE THE FACTS I HAVE STATED ARE TRUE.

_____	_____
Attorney/Plaintiff/Defendant	Date
_____	_____
Address	Telephone
_____	
City, State, Zip Code	

Serving a Motion

The original of every written motion must be filed with the clerk either before "*service*" or immediately thereafter.[109]

A copy of every written motion must be "*served*" on the other parties. Service of motions is less complicated than service of initial process. A motion is served when copies of the motion are delivered to the other parties or mailed to the other parties' last known addresses.[110] If a party is represented by an attorney, the motion should be sent to the attorney.[111]

A "*certificate of service*" should appear at the end of every motion (the certificate was redacted from the form above). The certificate of service simply confirms that the movant served a copy of the motion on the other parties or their attorneys. The certificate of service form is as follows:

CERTIFICATE OF SERVICE

I certify that a copy hereof has been furnished to (here insert name or names and address or addresses) by (delivery) (mail) (e-mail if an attorney) on .....(date)......

_____

(Party or party's attorney)

---

[109] Fla. Sm. Cl. R. 7.080(c).
[110] Fla. Sm. Cl. R. 7.080(b).
[111] *Id.*

16

DISMISSAL OF ONE'S OWN CLAIMS

If a plaintiff wishes to abandon his claim or a defendant his counterclaim, he must voluntarily dismiss it. Except in a case where property has been seized or is in the court's custody, a plaintiff may voluntarily dismiss his claim or a defendant may dismiss his counterclaim before it is submitted to the judge or jury for decision. There are two ways to accomplish a voluntary dismissal:

1. By informing the other parties and the clerk of the dismissal, or

2. By filing a stipulation of dismissal signed by all parties.[112]

A voluntary dismissal is "*without prejudice,*" unless the dismissing party states otherwise or unless it is the second time the claim was dismissed.[113] "Without prejudice" generally means that the claim or counterclaim might be asserted again at some point in the future. "With *prejudice*" means that the dismissing party is barred from bringing the dismissed claim again.

If a plaintiff dismisses all of his claims and a defendant has a pending counterclaim, the court will not dismiss the plaintiff's claims over defendant's objections unless the counterclaim will be able

---

[112] Fla. Sm. Cl. R. 7.110(a).
[113] *Id.*

to proceed independently. A defendant's voluntary dismissal of his counterclaim does not have any impact upon the plaintiff's statement of claim.

Dismissing a claim can have costly consequences and, therefore, it should only be done after thoughtful consideration. If a party is dismissing his claim for a second time, he must understand that he may be barred from ever bringing the claim again. Also, a party needs to be aware that if he dismisses his claim, he will likely have to pay the other party's court costs, if any.[114] Finally, if a party dismisses his claim and the dispute is based upon a contract, there could be a contractual provision that allows the opposing party to recover his attorneys' fees.

---

[114] Fla. Sm. Cl. R. 7.110(d).

17

DISMISSING THE OTHER PARTY'S CLAIMS

Failure to Comply

If the opposing party has failed to comply with the Florida Small Claims Rules or any order of the court, a party may serve a motion asking the court to dismiss the opposing party's claim.[115] If possible, it is best to prepare a written motion as outlined in the *Motions* section above and explain how the opposing party failed to comply and how the movant was adversely affected by the opposing party's non-compliance. But, dismissing a claim is an extraordinary action and the court is not very likely to do it unless the opposing party's actions were also extraordinary. Before filing a motion to dismiss based upon the other party's failure to comply with the Rules or a court order, a movant should carefully consider how seriously he has been harmed by the opposing party's non-compliance, how flagrant was the non-compliant party's disobedience, and how the motion may be perceived by the judge.

Failure to Present Sufficient Evidence

A party may also be able to dismiss the opposing party's claim through a motion for involuntary dismissal[116] if, after the opposing party's presentation of his evidence at the trial, the opposing party has not

---

[115] Fla. Sm. Cl. R. 7.110(b).

[116] If the motion is presented in a jury trial, it is called a motion for directed verdict.

presented sufficient evidence to establish his claim.[117] The motion is presented after the opposing party has presented the evidence supporting his claim, but before the movant presents his evidence in defense. Thus, this motion is nearly always made orally. Generally speaking, the motion attempts to argue that the opposing party has failed to establish his case as a matter of law. The court may not consider the weight of the evidence or the credibility of the witnesses in ruling on a motion for involuntary dismissal.[118] For example, as noted above in the *Stating a Legal Claim* section, if the opposing party has asserted a claim for breach of contract, he must establish certain facts, including that the parties entered into a contract. If the opposing party fails to present any evidence to show that there was a contract, then he has failed to establish his claim as a matter of law and a motion for involuntary dismissal is appropriate.

Failure to Prosecute

If there has been no activity—no motions, pleadings, notices, or orders—in the case for a period of six months, the case may be dismissed for lack of prosecution. The court acting on its own initiative or in response to a motion served by anyone—a party or a stranger to the case—may dismiss the action based upon the plaintiff's failure to prosecute the action upon 30 days' advance notice to the parties.[119]

At the hearing on a motion to dismiss based upon a failure to prosecute, the court will dismiss the case unless:

1. A stipulation staying the action has been filed with the court,

2. A stay order has been filed, or

3. A plaintiff shows good cause in writing at least five days before the hearing on the motion why the action should remain pending.

---

[117] Fla. Sm. Cl. R. 7.110(b).

[118] *See Brockman v. Brockman*, 788 So. 2d 416 (Fla. 1st DCA 2001).

[119] Fla. Sm. Cl. R. 7.110(e).

18

THE TRIAL

Having one's case decided by another human being who may deny the relief sought is to stare into the abyss.[120] Trials can be nerve-racking and the primary reason for that is the fear that the judge who hears and rules on the case will do so without knowledge, understanding, depth, or concern.[121] There are, however, several things that one can do to minimize the realization of this fear and to maximize the chances for success at trial.

Preparing for Trial
Although small claims trials are generally informal proceedings with the judge simply trying to get the facts he needs to make a decision, a party's pre-trial preparation bears a direct correlation to his ability to prove his case or establish his defense.

Witnesses
Witnesses are individuals or representatives of businesses or organizations who come to court to state, under oath, what they have seen, heard, touched, tasted, or smelled. Witnesses either have personal knowledge of some fact or circumstance at issue in the case or are experts on some subject matter involved in the case. An expert witness can be someone who has specialized education on a topic or it can be someone who,

---

[120] Peter R. Bornstein, *Persuading a Cold Judge*, Litigation, Winter 2009, p. 27.
[121] *Id.*

through training, skill, or experience, has more knowledge about a matter than the average person such as a mechanic or contractor.

The parties, more than likely, will be witnesses at the trial. The best practice is, however, to have other witnesses appear at trial to help a party prove his side of the case. Non-parties can be more persuasive than parties because, generally speaking, they have less of a stake in the outcome of the trial.

Another best practice is to talk to potential witnesses as soon possible. Parties should talk to their respective potential witnesses before the pretrial conference to ensure that the witnesses are willing to later testify at a trial because the availability or unavailability of witnesses at trial may be a factor in deciding whether and how to settle the case during mediation. Parties should talk to their respective witnesses again after the pretrial conference because the parties have now learned more about the case and will want to ensure that the witnesses are available at the date and time scheduled for the trial. If an important witness is not available for trial, a party should serve a motion asking the court to delay the trial to a time when the witness will be available because, generally speaking, affidavits are not admissible as evidence.

After the pre-trial conference, parties should also cause subpoenas to be served on all witnesses —even those who insist they will appear at trial without a subpoena. Witnesses should always be served with a subpoena to appear for trial. First, the subpoenas remind the witnesses of the trial date and time and reinforce the fact that the trial is an important event. Second, subpoenas provide witnesses with an "excuse" for their employers so that they might leave their work and attend the trial. Third and most importantly, serving subpoenas on witnesses may enable a party to convince the court to postpone or continue the trial if a witness, who is under subpoena, fails to appear to testify.

The best practice is to alert witnesses to the fact that they will be receiving subpoenas for trial. "Subpoena" means "under penalty," and subpoenas are threatening documents. Parties do not want their witnesses upset by the service of a subpoena; it's not a nice surprise. Likewise, parties should avoid another source of potential witness aggravation by not waiting until the last minute to serve the subpoenas. Even though the case is very important to the parties, it is unlikely that the case is as important to witnesses. Subpoenas should be served with sufficient time for witnesses to make appropriate arrangements to appear for trial.

Last, but certainly not least, witnesses should be told that subpoenas need to be served by the Sheriff's office or a private process server. Given the relatively short period of time between the pretrial conference and the trial however, the best practice is to have a private process server handle service of witness subpoenas.

Subpoena forms may be obtained from the clerk's offices, who will charge a fee for issuing the subpoenas. As reflected in the model subpoena below, the subpoena, when properly completed, provides the issuing court's name, the case caption, and commands the recipient to appear at a certain date and time to testify. Clerks generally sign and seal the subpoena forms, but they do not complete the other parts of the subpoena. Therefore, the party requesting the subpoena needs to carefully complete the subpoena form to, among other things, properly identify the witness' name and address.

An example of a subpoena form is as follows:

KURT E. LEE, ESQ. & TIM W. SOBCZAK, ESQ.

IN THE CIRCUIT/COUNTY COURT IN AND FOR CITRUS COUNTY
FIFTH JUDICIAL CIRCUIT OF FLORIDA

CASE NO.

Plaintiff(s)

-vs-

Defendant(s)
_____/

SUBPOENA

TO THE STATE OF FLORIDA:

TO: _____

    YOU ARE COMMANDED to appear before the Honorable _____,
Circuit/County Court Judge, at the Citrus County Courthouse, in Inverness, Florida, on
_____, 20____, at _____ A.M./P.M., to testify in the above-styled cause. If you
fail to appear you may be in contempt of Court.

    You are subpoenaed to appear by _____
and unless excused from this subpoena by same or by the Court, you shall respond to this subpoena as directed.

    WITNESS my hand and the seal of this court on this ____day of _____, A.D.,
20____.

                  ANGELA VICK
                  CLERK OF THE COURT

                  By:_____
                      Deputy Clerk

IF YOU ARE A PERSON WITH A DISABILITY WHO NEEDS ANY ACCOMMODATION IN ORDER TO PARTICIPATE IN THIS PROCEEDING, YOU ARE
ENTITLED, AT NO COST TO YOU, TO THE PROVISION OF CERTAIN ASSISTANCE. PLEASE CONTACT THE ADA COORDINATOR, TELEPHONE
(352)-341-6700, CITRUS COUNTY COURTHOUSE, 110 N APOPKA AVENUE, INVERNESS FL 34450, WITHIN 2 WORKING DAYS OF YOUR RECEIPT OF
THIS SUBPOENA. IF YOU ARE HEARING OR VOICE IMPAIRED, CALL 1-800-955-2771

C:/COUNTY/FORMS/SUBPOENA/WITNESS/0303

Documents

At trial, some documents and things are essential to your case. For example, a contractor seeking to be paid for work will need to have his contractor's license. For another example, a case involving the alleged breach of a written contract requires that the contract be introduced into evidence at the trial. But documents and things may also be used to support or discredit what a witness is saying. For example, if a witness testifies that something appears one way, a picture or video might be used to show that it appears another.

The best practice with respect to documents and things is to collect and organize them as soon as possible. Parties should review their documents and things prior to the pretrial conference to determine the probative value of the materials and to analyze whether additional documents might be necessary for trial and whether such documents might be readily obtained.

If a party needs documents or things that are not in his possession, he can serve a subpoena on a business or individual who has the necessary material to bring such material to the trial. The suggestions above regarding the best practices for dealing with witnesses and subpoenas for trials applies with equal force here.

The Day of Trial

The parties need to be present for the trial. The best practice is to arrive early and to be ready when the judge calls the case. A case might be dismissed if the plaintiff is absent or a judgment might be summarily entered if the defendant is absent.

Judges hearing small claims cases generally schedule several trials for the same trial period. Judges schedule more than one trial at a time because cases often settle "on the courthouse steps" and judges seek to avoid having unused trial time: if one case settles, then there is another one ready to take its place. Parties should plan on spending twice as long at the courthouse as they think the trial will require. Most small claims trials take less than one hour, but the length of any particular trial will be dependent upon the nature of the dispute and the number of witnesses.

The parties should dress professionally. If a judge sees that a party is dressed in a professional manner, the judge is more inclined to believe that the party is organized and prepared for the proceeding. Parties should also advise their witnesses to dress professionally.

Be polite and courteous at all times. Do not interrupt the judge, other parties, or any of the witnesses. There certainly should be no shouting or name-calling during the trial.[122] Throughout the trial, address the judge as "judge" or "your honor" and address the parties or witnesses formally, e.g., "Mr. Smith."

Conducting the Trial

As at the pretrial conference, cases will be called and the parties will need to come before the judge.

If all of the parties are without lawyers, the judge will usually ask the parties to also have their respective witnesses come forward. The judge or his courtroom clerk will then place all of the parties and their witnesses under oath. Given the time pressure associated with small claims trials, it is uncommon for parties and witnesses to be individually placed under oath and to testify from a witness box.

The judge might then take the lead and start asking the parties about the case or he might invite the parties to make opening statements. In either event, it is important to keep in mind that the county judges who oversee small claims trials are very busy. It is highly unlikely that the judge overseeing the trial has any familiarity with the case —even if the judge heard something about the case at the pretrial conference. Thus, the parties cannot simply pick-up where they left off at the pretrial conference and resume talking about their respective positions.

---

[122] Indeed, if a party defames another party in a small claims action, he might be subject to a later action for damages if such defamatory words are not connected with or relevant to the cause at hand or subject of inquiry. *See Goodman v. Goldstein*, 145 So. 2d 882 (Fla. 3d DCA 1962).

It is also important to be mindful that county judges are generalists: county judges do not specialize in real estate leases, construction contracts, automobile negligence cases, or whatever area of the law the particular small claims case involves.[123] Thus, the best practice is to not assume that the judge knows the law that applies to the case or what is "normal" or "customary" in a particular industry.

Accordingly, the best practice at trial is to begin at the beginning and to ensure that the following six basic questions are answered for the judge either in response to the judge's explicit questions or as part of the opening statement: Who are you? Who is with you? What is the controversy, in one sentence? Why are you here? What outcome or relief do you want? Why should you get it?[124] These questions and their answers are so important that the answers should be written on a pad or note cards so that reference might be made to them no matter how nervous one might become.

If the judge has had the parties give opening statements, he will then invite the parties to call any witnesses they have. If the judge has opted to ask questions of the parties, he might then ask the parties if they have anything further to add. In either event, this is the time for parties to call their witnesses and provide the court with any documents and things that support their claims or defenses. The plaintiff will have the first opportunity to call his witnesses.

Calling Witnesses

The parties are witnesses. Thus, if the plaintiff has not already testified on his behalf, he should do so. Although the order in which witnesses may be called is a strategy decision for the parties, it is probably best for the plaintiff to be his first witness due to the primacy effect. People tend to remember the first information presented about something better than information presented later —and that rule applies to judges as much as anyone else. The plaintiff usually has the most information

---

[123] Bornstein, *supra*, note 122.
[124] *Id.*

about his case and, thus, should take advantage of the primacy effect by being the first voice heard by the judge.

The plaintiff's testimony may be in the form of a narrative; the plaintiff should tell the story about the case. A plaintiff should not ask himself questions. If the plaintiff has not already answered the six queries described above, he should do so now being sure to pay particular attention to the elements of the claim and the relief sought. If the plaintiff has any information about the dispute that he wants to share with the judge, he should do so as part of his initial testimony.

After the plaintiff is done testifying, the defendant, if permitted by the judge, may have the opportunity to "*cross-examine*" the plaintiff. If permitted, the defendant will ask the plaintiff questions intended to bolster the defendant's defenses or claims, undermine the plaintiff's assertions, and/or demonstrate that the plaintiff is an unreliable witness. Trial judges generally monitor cross-examination of the parties carefully to ensure that the questions and answers do not devolve into an argument: the judge knows that the plaintiff and defendant disagree because they are appearing before him for a trial! If a plaintiff is cross-examined, then he will have an opportunity for "re-direct" and to "rebut" or explain any points raised by the defendant during cross-examination.

Following the plaintiff's testimony, the plaintiff might then call his witnesses. If there is more than one witness, the best approach is probably to call the witnesses so that their testimony is consistent with the chronology of the matter. In other words, if Witness "A" knows something about the first part of the dispute and Witness "B" knows something about a later aspect of the dispute, Witness "A" should probably be called before Witness "B."

Witness testimony usually requires the plaintiff to ask questions of the witness. A plaintiff should begin each "*examination*" by asking the witness to state his name. A witness should then be asked a question to elicit an answer that shows how the witness has knowledge of the dispute. For example, if a mail clerk is being called to testify that a payment was not received, the witness might be asked how he was employed during the pertinent time period. This foundational question will help the judge understand how this witness knows the payment was not received. After these introductory questions are asked, the plaintiff should then ask questions of the witness that directly support the plaintiff's case.

Do not interrupt witnesses even if you think information provided by a witness is inaccurate or needs clarification. Interrupting witnesses will be perceived as rudeness by the judge and efforts to clarify testimony before the witness is finished speaking will be perceived as "*coaching*" and will undermine the witness's credibility. The best practice is to allow the witness to complete his answer and to then ask follow up questions to ensure that testimony is accurate and clear. Indeed, interrupting a witness is really only proper when a party believes he has an allowable objection.

After the witness answers the plaintiff's questions, the defendant may be permitted to cross-examine. The defendant will ask the witness questions intended to bolster his claims or defenses, undermine the plaintiff's claims, and/or demonstrate that the witness is unreliable. It is more likely that the judge will permit cross-examination of witnesses who are not parties to the action. After the defendant completes his cross-examination, the plaintiff will then have the opportunity to "*re-direct*" the witness and ask questions to address any points made during the cross-examination.

After the plaintiff and his witnesses have finished testifying, the defendant will be given an opportunity to testify and call his witnesses. Although the same procedure described above can be followed, defendants should consider the recency effect. People – of which your judge is one – tend to remember the most recent information presented above other information. Thus, a defendant may decide that, as a result of the recency effect, to call other witnesses and, then, testify as the last witness.

Witnesses Appearing by Telephone

Although the best practice is for parties and witnesses to be present before the judge, judges have the discretion to permit testimony from any party or witness to be presented by telephone. Thus, parties who have witnesses who cannot appear for the trial might serve a motion as soon as they learn of the witnesses' unavailability and request permission for telephone appearances. Again, affidavits and written statements from witnesses are not admissible as evidence —parties and witnesses need to provide their testimony during the trial.

Objections

An objection is a statement opposing something that has occurred, or is about to occur, in court based upon the Florida Evidence Code.[125] An objection seeks the judge's immediate ruling on a matter. Although Florida's Evidence Code can sometimes be complicated, in small claims matters the judge will often treat the Code as a "guide" as opposed to rules and allow the parties greater leeway to facilitate the presentation of evidence.[126] Nevertheless, it is sometimes appropriate to object to evidence.

Objections are made orally and should be concise. If a party has an objection to some testimony or document or thing, a party should state, "Objection," with sufficient volume to be heard and, then, briefly state the basis for the objection. For example, if a party is asking his billing clerk for the third time whether an account was paid, the other party might state, "Objection. Asked and answered." After stating an objection, the objecting party should listen for the judge's ruling. If the judge says, "Sustained," the objection has been granted and the evidence should not be admitted. If the judge says, "Denied" or "Overruled," the objection has not been granted and, absent any further objections, the evidence will be admitted.

A party's or witnesses' testimony, documents, and things are not objectionable because they might be harmful or prejudicial to the

---

[125] *See* Black's Law Dictionary 500 (3d ed. 2006). The Florida Evidence Code can be found in Chapter 90, *Florida Statutes.*

[126] *See* Fla. Sm. Cl. R. 7.140(f).

other party. Indeed, each party is attempting to have evidence at trial that helps his case and hurts the other party's case.

Evidence is, however, objectionable if it falls within the scope of the following:

1. **"Asked and answered"** - It is unfair and unnecessary to ask a witness questions that have already been answered by the witness.[127] It is appropriate, however, to inquire if a witness is sure about his testimony or to clarify some aspect of the witness's testimony.

2. **"Beyond the scope"** - A party who is cross-examining a witness is generally restricted to asking questions concerning subjects that were addressed during direct examination.[128] If the party would like to ask questions "beyond the scope," he is normally required to recall the witness during his part of the case. Because of the leeway given during small claims matters, this objection will rarely be successful in a small claims case.

3. **"Hearsay"** - Although leeway is given in small claims cases, "hearsay" is a form of evidence that will often be excluded by the judge. Hearsay is an out of court statement that is offered for the truth of the matter asserted.[129] For example, if a party asks one of his witnesses to tell the judge what a police officer told him about the cause of an accident or if a witness starts talking about what he heard about an incident, the other party should object on the basis of "hearsay."

There are exceptions to the hearsay rule. The most common exception in small claims cases is an out of court statement by a party.[130]

---

[127] § 90.612(1), Fla. Stat. (2013).

[128] § 90.612(2), Fla. Stat. (2013). However, witnesses may generally always testify as to the opposing party's credibility.

[129] *See* § 90.801, Fla. Stat. (2013).

[130] *See* § 90.803(18), Fla. Stat. (2013).

A party and his witnesses are, generally speaking, permitted to testify about what the other party or his agents said outside of the courtroom.

In addition to testimony, documents and things might also be objectionable on the basis of hearsay. Indeed, it is the ban against hearsay that prevents affidavits or witness statements from being admitted into evidence. Repair bills, contractor estimates, and work orders are examples of documents and things which contain out of court statements and which may be excluded from evidence upon objection.

There are, however, exceptions to the hearsay rule that also apply to documents. The most common exception involving documents in small claims matters is the business records exception. Generally speaking, a party needing to introduce documents and things into evidence must have someone from the business with knowledge of the business's record keeping practices attend the trial and attest to the method by which the business records were created and their accuracy.[131]

4. **"Irrelevant"** - Evidence or testimony must tend to prove or disprove a material fact.[132] Thus, a party in a case involving a dispute over a dry cleaning invoice might object if the other party attempts to ask his ex-wife if he is current on child support obligations.

5. **"Leading"** - A party may not ask his own witness a question that suggests an answer.[133] For example, a party may not ask his own witness, "The car then turned to the left, correct?" But, leading of witnesses is permitted, and even encouraged, on cross-examination. Because of the leeway given during small claims case, this objection will rarely be successful.

---

[131] § 90.803(6), Fla. Stat. (2013).

[132] § 90.401, Fla. Stat. (2013).

[133] § 90.612(3), Fla. Stat. (2013).

6. **"Speculation"** - Witnesses may not speculate and may only testify concerning matters to which they have personal knowledge.[134]

Conclusion of the Trial

At the end of the trial, the judge may announce his decision. If, however, the trial was complicated or the parties displayed anger toward each other, the judge might decide to take some additional time to review the evidence or research case law before he announces his final judgment. When the judge delays announcing his ruling, he will often say that he is taking the matter "under advisement." If the judge takes the case under advisement, he will subsequently mail the parties a copy of the final judgment.

If either party is disappointed with the results of the trial, he may file a written "*motion for a new trial.*" A motion for new trial asks the court to conduct a new trial based upon some error in the original trial.[135] A motion for new trial must be filed no later than 10 days after the return of a verdict in a jury trial or the date of filing of the judgment in a bench trial. [136] A judge will usually rule upon a motion for new trial without the necessity of a hearing.

A disappointed party also has the right to appeal a judgment to the circuit court. There will be a new filing fee and other costs involved with filing an appeal. Because the procedures for appealing a judgment are particular and detailed, an attorney should be consulted.

Court Reporter

Most small claims trials result in a judgment that is neither appealed nor subjected to any further scrutiny by the court. The reason for this lack of post-judgment review is primarily economical: it rarely makes sense from a costs/benefits perspective for parties to spend more time and money on a small claims matter regardless of its outcome.

---

[134] § 90.604, Fla. Stat. (2013).

[135] Fla. Sm. Cl. R. 7.180.

[136] *Id.*

However, if the stakes of the small claims case are such that appellate review might ultimately be necessary, then a court reporter should be retained to be present at the trial to transcribe the proceedings. Appellate courts generally require trial transcripts so that they might review what happened at trial and decide whether the trial judge correctly ruled.[137] Indeed, appellate courts usually presume that the "trial court's decision is correct unless the appellant provides the appellate court with a record that is sufficient to evaluate the appellant's contentions of error."[138]

Court reporters may be found in any Florida county. Most court reporters charge a nominal fee for appearing at hearings and trials. If a transcript is necessary, court reporters then charge a "per page" fee for such transcription.

---

[137] *Pierson v. Sharp*, 283 So. 2d 880, 881-82 (Fla. 4th DCA 1973)("Although we are not unsympathetic to petitioner's argument that the Small Claims Court is 'the peoples' court' wherein court reporters are not customarily utilized, this fact can not justify an appellate court in ignoring or discarding its proper appellate role.").

[138] *Harrison v. Harrison*, 909 So. 2d 318, 319 (Fla. 2d DCA 2004).

19

FINAL JUDGMENT

The final judgment is a very important document because it memorializes the trial result. Although the judge usually prepares the judgment, the parties should carefully review it to ensure that it reflects the judge's ruling and is accurate. Errors or inaccuracies should be brought to the trial judge's attention immediately through a motion expressing the requested relief.

A form final judgment for a money judgment against a defendant is as follows:

(CAPTION)

FINAL JUDGMENT AGAINST

(DEFENDANT(S)'S NAME)

It is adjudged that the plaintiff, (name and address), recover from the defendant, (name, address, and social security number), the sum of $_____ on principal, $_____ as prejudgment interest, with costs of $_____, all of which shall bear interest at the rate of ____% per year as provided by Florida Statute, for all of which let execution issue.

It is further ordered and adjudged that the defendant(s) shall complete Florida Small Claims Rules Form 7.343 (Fact Information Sheet) and return it to the plaintiff's attorney, or to the plaintiff if the plaintiff is not represented by an attorney, within 45 days from the date of this final judgment, unless the final judgment is satisfied or a motion for new trial or notice of appeal is filed. The defendant should NOT file the completed form 7.343 with the court. Jurisdiction of this case is retained to enter further orders that are proper to compel the defendant(s) to complete from 7.343 and return it to the plaintiff's attorney, or the plaintiff if the plaintiff is not represented by an attorney.

ORDERED at _____, Florida, on (date)

_____
County Court Judge

Copies furnished to:
Plaintiff
Defendant

The applicable interest rate, if not specified in a contract between the parties, can be obtained from www.myfloridacfo.com, Florida's Chief Financial Officer's website.[139] "Costs" in the above form refers to specified costs that Florida law deems recoverable by the prevailing party. Typically, the only recoverable costs in a small claims case are the filing fee and the service of process fee.

The judgment should always contain the plaintiff's address and, if known, the defendant's address and social security number.[140] If, however, this information is omitted, it may be provided by an affidavit, which will be recorded along with the judgment. In other words, there is no need to file and serve a motion asking the judge to insert this missing information.

---

[139] Florida's Chief Financial Officer is required to set the rate of interest payable on judgments and decrees on December 1, March 1, June 1, and September 1 of each year for the following applicable quarter. § 55.03(1), Fla. Stat. (2013).

[140] §§ 55.01(2) and 55.10(1), Fla. Stat. (2013).

If the party against whom the judgment is entered fails to pay or perform the obligations imposed by such judgment, the party in whose favor the judgment was entered will need to take action to "*enforce*" the judgment. The court will not enforce the judgment on its own accord. If a judgment debtor does not pay a judgment, the judgment creditor will need to discover the debtor's assets and then take further actions to seize such assets to satisfy the judgment. (Thus, the "*enforcement paragraph*," the second paragraph in the above final judgment form, is a significant benefit to a judgment creditor because it helps reveal such assets.)

20

COLLECTING ON JUDGMENTS

Most small claims judgments involve the payment of money. The court enters a judgment requiring one party to pay a sum to another. If, however, the judgment debtor, the party who is obliged to pay, does not voluntarily pay the judgment creditor, the party in whose favor the judgment was entered, then the judgment creditor will need to take other actions to satisfy his judgment. The court will not collect the money owed to a judgment creditor for the judgment creditor.

Obtaining a Judgment Lien

A judgment creditor might obtain a judgment lien on the debtor's property. A judgment lien acts as a *"cloud"* on the title of the debtor's property. Obtaining a judgment lien is necessary to establish the judgment creditor's priority or position vis-a-vis other individuals who or businesses which might have liens against the debtor. The sooner a judgment creditor obtains a judgment lien, the better.

Real Property

To obtain a judgment lien on the debtor's real property—lands and buildings—a judgment creditor must record a certified copy of the judgment in the county where the real property is located. If the parties' addresses and the debtor's social security or taxpayer identification number are not already included in the judgment, an affidavit containing such information needs to be recorded with the judgment.

The clerk in the county where the case was filed will automatically record a copy of the judgment in the public records. But, this recorded judgment is not a certified copy of the judgment, and it is the recordation of a certified copy of the judgment that creates the lien. Accordingly, the judgment creditor should obtain a certified copy of the judgment from the clerk and then cause such copy to be recorded. A certified copy will have a stamp or notation on the judgment whereby the clerk "*certifies*" that it is a "*true copy*" of the judgment. A certified copy of the judgment must be recorded in every Florida county in which the judgment debtor owns property to be a lien on the property.

After the certified copy of the judgment is recorded, the judgment debtor must first satisfy the judgment lien if he wants to sell the property.

Properties owned by a judgment debtor might be revealed in the fact information sheet or through each county's real property records. A county's public records and the county's property appraiser's records are usually accessible via the Internet.

Judgment liens are valid for an initial period of 10 years.[141] If the full amount of the judgment has not been collected within 10 years, the lien might be extended for an additional 10 year period by: (a) re-recording a certified copy of the judgment prior to the expiration of the initial 10 year period; (b) if the parties' addresses and the debtor's social security or taxpayer identification number is not already included in the judgment (An affidavit containing such information needs to be simultaneously recorded with the re-recorded judgment); and (c) an affidavit with the address of the lien's current owner must also be simultaneously recorded with the re-recorded judgment. Judgment liens can only be extended once and are, therefore, only valid for a maximum of 20 years or until paid in full, whichever occurs first.

Personal Property

To obtain a lien on the judgment debtor's personal property—movable objects other than money and negotiable instruments—a

---

[141] § 55.10, Fla. Stat. (2013).

judgment debtor must record a Judgment Lien Certificate with the Florida Department of State. This process can be accomplished via the Internet, and the forms might be obtained at www.sunbiz.org or by calling the Department of State at (850) 245-6039. A lien on the judgment debtor's personal property is effective statewide.

Execution

A writ of execution is a command to the sheriff directing him to seize, advertise, and sell to the highest bidder, the judgment debtor's personal property. The proceeds of the sale will be used first to satisfy the costs incurred with seizing, advertising, and selling of the property and second to satisfy the judgment. A sheriff may continue to seize and sell the judgment debtor's property until the full amount of the judgment plus the costs are paid.

A writ of execution may be obtained from the clerk of the county that issued the judgment. After receiving the writ, a judgment debtor must deliver it and a clerk-provided form entitled "Instructions for Levy" to the sheriff's office where the property is located. The instructions for levy describe the property to be seized and direct the sheriff's deputies to where the property might be found.

Judgment creditors are required to advance the costs necessary to seize, store, advertise, and sell the property. These advances are considered costs, which you are entitled to recover from the defendant out of the proceeds of the sale. Sometimes the defendant will pay the judgment immediately after the property is seized. Frequently, the most accessible personal property to seize is an automobile. Information regarding the defendant's automobile(s) should be on the fact information sheet; however, if you have not received the fact information sheet or you believe its information is inaccurate, you can obtain vehicle registration and licensing information by writing the Department of Highway Safety and Motor Vehicles, Division of Motor Vehicles, Neil Kirkman Building, Tallahassee, Florida 32399-0500.

Garnishment

Garnishment is the taking of property of a defendant that is in the hands of a third party, the garnishee, and applying the property to satisfy the judgment. The plaintiff secures by garnishment the right to have the debt owed by the garnishee to the defendant paid by the garnishee to the plaintiff.

Perhaps the most familiar form of garnishment is the process by which the plaintiff attaches the wages of the defendant, compelling the employer (garnishee) to turn earnings over to the plaintiff.

Note: Earnings subject to garnishment are limited to 25% of the defendant's disposable earnings (earnings after taxes and social security withholdings) for that week, or the amount by which his/her disposable earnings for that week exceed 30 times the federal minimum hourly wage in effect at the time the wages are payable, whichever is less.

Garnishment is not limited to wages. Any money, chattels (articles of personal property) or effects of the defendant held by a third party may be subject to garnishment. Money in bank accounts may be garnished, as may household furnishings, automobiles, or any type of personal property that is in possession of someone other than the defendant. It should be noted that a defendant is entitled to certain exemptions that would effect a garnishment action if this option is being considered.

Exemptions

1. If determined by the Court to be the Head of a Household, the defendant's salary or wages would be exempt.

2. Land on which the defendant makes his/her homestead.

3. One thousand ($1,000.00) worth of personal property.

If you wish to proceed with a garnishment action, you would file a Motion for Garnishment (obtained from the Summary Claims Division, Office of the Clerk of the Court). There is a fee involved for filing a Garnishment Action. However, you are entitled to recover this fee from the defendant. Once filed, a Writ of Garnishment is issued to be served on the garnishee, along with "Notice to Defendant of Right Against Garnishment of Wages, Money and other Property"; and, "Claim of Exemption and Request for Hearing" forms. The garnishee would file an answer stating money owed the defendant or personal property being held, if any. Since, by law, you can recover only a percentage of the money each time you garnish, you may find it necessary to file several times before the entire amount of the judgment is recovered.

It should be noted that none of the remedies assure you of immediate recovery of the money due you from the judgment.

21

SATISFACTION OF JUDGMENT

When your Final Judgment is paid in full (i.e., satisfied), you are required to acknowledge, and record a Satisfaction of Judgment.[142] Within 60 days after the date of receipt of the full payment of the judgment, you must send the recorded Satisfaction of Judgment to the defendant.[143] The Satisfaction of Judgment form is available from the clerk of court's office.[144]

---

[142] § 701.04(2), Fla. Stat. (2013).

[143] *Id.*

[144] The form is also located in the Florida Small Claims Rules as Form 7.347.

22

WHAT IF I WANT TO APPEAL THE JUDGMENT?

Whether or not a party can appeal a particular small claims court decision, whether or not a party should appeal a small claims court decision, and when a party must file the notice of appeal can be complicated questions. Thus, parties should consult an attorney before making any decision concerning an appeal. However, the following are some appellate basics.

The circuit court has final appellate jurisdiction of all cases arising in the small claims court. The Florida Rules of Appellate Procedure govern the circuit court's review of a small claims court decision.[145] According to the Florida Rules of Appellate Procedure, to appeal a small claims court decision you must file a notice of appeal with the clerk of the circuit court and pay a filing fee.

The notice of appeal must typically be filed within 30 days of the date that the small claims court decision was filed with the clerk of court (not necessarily within 30 days of the date at the bottom of the order or judgment). The circuit court may review final orders, such as a final judgment discussed above, and some non-final orders, such as a court's decision concerning venue.

---

[145] Fla. Sm. Cl. R. 7.230.

23

SHOULD I HIRE AN ATTORNEY?

Parties do not need to hire an attorney to represent them in a Florida small claims case. Even corporations, which are usually required by Florida law to have an attorney represent them in legal proceedings, are permitted to appear in small claims lawsuits through an authorized non-lawyer designee and without an attorney.

Moreover, Florida's Small Claims Rules require clerks to assist the parties with the papers to be filed in a small claims lawsuit and direct judges to assist unrepresented parties with courtroom decorum and the order of presentation of evidence.

Thus, anyone who does not get too nervous speaking in public, who is organized and keeps accurate records, who has the time to prepare the necessary documents and attend court hearings, and who is comfortable negotiating with the other side or his attorney might opt to proceed without an attorney and with the likelihood of success.

On the other hand, the clerk's office and the judge can only help so much. Employees within the clerk's offices generally lack legal training and the judge cannot advise the parties on legal matters because he must remain impartial. Thus, it often makes sense to consult with an attorney and, if an action is not resolved at mediation, to have an attorney present at trial.

Moreover, it is worthwhile to consult with an attorney if:

a. A party does not know the legal basis for his claim;

b. A party wants legal advice about claims or defenses;

c. A party does not understand the papers he receives from the other party or the court;

d. A party cannot afford to lose the case; or

e. The case is complicated either because of the law, the number and location of documents, or the number and location of witnesses.

24

HOW SHOULD I SELECT AN ATTORNEY?

Hiring an attorney is similar to hiring any other service provider: seek referrals from trusted acquaintances and make a careful investigation of the prospective lawyers. Do not be afraid to request that attorneys provide information about their respective qualifications and experience such as:

a. The attorney's resume. An attorney's educational background, prior positions, special honors and recognitions, and certifications and specialized education might help differentiate among attorneys.

b. The attorney's experience with the subject matter of the small claims action.

c. The fees and costs to be charged and how they will be paid.

d. The on-line reputation of the attorney and law firm.

Selecting an attorney is an important decision. Attorney advertising sometimes complicates this decision, but there are a number of online resources that provide factual information upon which an intelligent hiring decision may be based.[146]

[146] *See, e.g.,* Steve Nohlgren, *Culpepper Kurland law firm long on image, short on trials,* Tampa Bay Times, Jan. 26, 2013, http://www.tampabay.com/news/courts/culpepper-kurland-law-firm-long-on-image-short-on-trials/1272324.

[APPENDIX]

Model Statements of Claims

1. Statement of Claim for Goods Sold
(CAPTION)

STATEMENT OF CLAIM

Plaintiff, _____, sues defendant, _____, and alleges: There is now due, owing, and unpaid from defendant to plaintiff $_____ with interest since _____, 20_____(date)____, for the following goods sold and delivered by plaintiff to defendant between _____, 20_____ (date)____, and _____, 20_____(date)____:

(list goods and prices and any credits)

WHEREFORE, plaintiff demands judgment for damages against defendant.

2. Statement of Claim for Work Done and Materials Furnished
(CAPTION)

STATEMENT OF CLAIM

Plaintiff, _____, sues defendant, _____, and alleges: There is now due, owing, and unpaid from defendant to plaintiff $_____ with interest since _____, 20_____(date)____, for the following items of labor and materials furnished to defendant at his/her request between _____, 20_____(date)____, and _____, 20_____ (date)____:

(list time and materials, showing charges therefor and any credits)

WHEREFORE, plaintiff demands judgment for damages against defendant.

3. Statement of Claim for Money Lent
(CAPTION)

STATEMENT OF CLAIM

Plaintiff, _____, sues defendant, _____, and alleges: There is now due, owing, and unpaid from defendant to plaintiff $_____ for money lent by plaintiff to defendant on _____, 20_____(date)____, with interest thereon since _____, 20_____(date)____

WHEREFORE, plaintiff demands judgment for damages against defendant.

4. Statement of Claim for Promissory Note
(CAPTION)

STATEMENT OF CLAIM

Plaintiff, _____, sues defendant, _____, and alleges:

1. This is an action for damages that do not exceed the sum of $5,000.

2. On _____, 20_____(date)____, defendant executed and delivered to plaintiff a promissory note, a copy being attached, in _____ County, Florida.

3. Defendant failed to pay

(a) the note when due; or

(b) the installment payment due on said note on _____, 20_____ (date) _____, and plaintiff elected to accelerate payment of the balance.

4. There is now due, owing, and unpaid from defendant to plaintiff $_____ on said note with interest since _____, 20_____(date)____

5. Plaintiff has obligated himself/herself to pay his/her attorneys a reasonable fee for their services in bringing this action.

WHEREFORE, plaintiff demands judgment for damages against defendant.

5. Statement of Claim for Automobile Negligence
(CAPTION)

STATEMENT OF CLAIM

The plaintiff sues the defendant and says: On or about ...., in the vicinity of ...., on a public highway in .... County, Florida, plaintiff's motor vehicle, being operated by ...., collided with defendant's motor vehicle, being operated by ....; and the collision with plaintiff's vehicle was caused by the negligent and careless operation of defendant's vehicle, whereby plaintiff's vehicle was damaged and depreciated in value.

WHEREFORE, plaintiff demands judgment in the sum of $..........[147]

---

[147] This form may be found as Florida Small Claims Rule, Form 7.330. Form 7.330 appears to require a plaintiff to specifically state the amount of damages sought despite the fact that proof of the automobile's depreciation will likely be in the form of opinions and be an issue of fact which will need to be decided by the judge or jury. Accordingly, it is suggested that plaintiffs using this form use this phrase instead, "WHEREFORE, plaintiff demands judgment for damages against defendant."

Florida Small Claims Rules (As of November 2013)

RULE 7.010. TITLE AND SCOPE

(a) **Title.** These rules shall be cited as Florida Small Claims Rules and may be abbreviated "Fla. Sm. Cl. R." These rules shall be construed to implement the simple, speedy, and inexpensive trial of actions at law in county courts.

(b) **Scope.** These rules are applicable to all actions at law of a civil nature in the county courts in which the demand or value of property involved does not exceed $5,000 exclusive of costs, interest, and attorneys' fees. If there is a difference between the time period prescribed by these rules and by section 51.011, Florida Statutes, the statutory provision shall govern.

RULE 7.020. APPLICABILITY OF RULES OF CIVIL PROCEDURE

(a) **Generally.** Florida Rules of Civil Procedure 1.090(a), (b), and (c); 1.190(e); 1.210(b); 1.260; 1.410; and 1.560 are applicable in all actions covered by these rules.

(b) **Discovery.** Any party represented by an attorney is subject to discovery pursuant to Florida Rules of Civil Procedure 1.280–1.380 directed at said party, without order of court. If a party proceeding without an attorney directs discovery to a party represented by an attorney, the represented party may also use discovery pursuant to the above-mentioned rules without leave of court. When a party is unrepresented and has not initiated discovery pursuant to Florida Rules of Civil Procedure 1.280–1.380, the opposing party shall not be entitled to initiate such discovery without leave of court. However, the time for such discovery procedures may be prescribed by the court.

(c) **Additional Rules.** In any particular action, the court may order that action to proceed under 1 or more additional Florida Rules of Civil Procedure on application of any party or the stipulation of all parties or on the court's own motion.

RULE 7.040. CLERICAL AND ADMINISTRATIVE DUTIES OF CLERK

(a) **Generally.** The clerk of the circuit court or the clerk of the county court in those counties where such a clerk is provided (hereinafter referred to as the clerk) shall:

(1) maintain a trial calendar. The placing of any action thereon with the date and time of trial is notice to all concerned of the order in which they may expect such action to be called;

(2) maintain a docket book and a judgment book (which may be the same book) in which accurate entries of all actions brought before the court and notations of the proceedings shall comply with Florida Rule of Judicial Administration 2.425 and shall be made including the date of filing; the date of issuance, service,

and return of process; the appearance of such parties as may appear; the fact of trial, whether by court or jury; the issuance of execution and to whom issued and the date thereof and return thereon and, when satisfied, a marginal entry of the date thereof; the issuance of a certified copy; a memorandum of the items of costs including witness fees; and the record of the verdict of the jury or finding of the judge, and the judgment, including damages and costs, which judgments may be kept in a separate judgment book; and

(3) maintain an alphabetical index by parties' names with reference to action and case number.

(b) Minute Book. It shall not be necessary for the clerk to maintain a minute book for small claims.

RULE 7.050. COMMENCEMENT OF ACTION; STATEMENT OF CLAIM

(a) Commencement.

(1) *Statement of Claim.* Actions are commenced by the filing of a statement of claim in concise form, which shall inform the defendant of the basis and the amount of the claim. If the claim is based on a written document, a copy or the material part thereof shall be attached to the statement of claim. All documents served upon the defendant with initial process shall be filed with the court.

(2) *Party Not Represented by Attorney to Sign.* A party, individual, or corporation who or which has no attorney handling such cause shall sign that party's statement of claim or other paper and state that party's address and telephone number, including area code, and may include

an e-mail address. However, if the trial court in its discretion determines that the plaintiff is engaged in the business of collecting claims and holds such claim being sued upon by purchase, assignment, or management arrangement in the operation of such business, the court may require that corporation to provide counsel in the prosecution of the cause. A corporation may be represented at any stage of the trial court proceedings by an officer of the corporation or any employee authorized in writing by an officer of the corporation.

(b) Parties. The names, addresses, and telephone numbers, including area code, of all parties or their attorneys, if any, must be stated on the statement of claim. A party not represented by an attorney may include an e-mail address. Additionally, attorneys must include their Florida Bar number on all papers filed with the court, as well as an e-mail address, in compliance with the Florida Rules of Judicial Administration.

(c) Clerk's Duties. The clerk shall assist in the preparation of a statement of claim and other papers to be filed in the action at the request of any litigant. The clerk shall not be required to prepare papers on constructive service, substituted service, proceedings supplementary to execution, or discovery procedures.

(d) Memorandum on Hearing Date. The court shall furnish all parties with a memorandum of the day and hour set for the hearing.

(e) Replevin. In those replevin cases to which these rules are applicable, the clerk of the county court shall set the hearing required by section 78.065(2)(a), Florida Statutes (prejudgment replevin order to show cause hearings) and rule 7.050(d) (pretrial conferences) at the same time.

RULE 7.060. PROCESS AND VENUE

(a) Summons Required. A summons entitled Notice to Appear stating the time and place of hearing shall be served on the defendant. The summons or notice to appear shall inform the defendant, in a separate paragraph containing bold type, of the defendant's right of venue. This paragraph on venue shall read:

Right to Venue. The law gives the person or company who has sued you the right to file suit in any one of several places as listed below. However, if you have been sued in any place other than one of these places, you, as the defendant, have the right to request that the case be moved to a proper location or venue. A proper location or venue may be one of the following:

1. Where the contract was entered into.

2. If the suit is on an unsecured promissory note, where the note is signed or where the maker resides.

3. If the suit is to recover property or to foreclose a lien, where the property is located.

4. Where the event giving rise to the suit occurred.

5. Where any one or more of the defendants sued reside.

6. Any location agreed to in a contract.

7. In an action for money due, if there is no agreement as to where suit may be filed, where payment is to be made.

If you, as a defendant, believe the plaintiff has not sued in one of these correct places, you must appear on your court date and orally request a transfer, or you must file a written request for transfer in affidavit form (sworn to under oath) with the court 7 days prior to your first court date and send a copy to the plaintiff or plaintiff's attorney, if any.

(b) Copy of Claim to Be Served. A copy of the statement of claim shall be served with the summons/notice to appear.

RULE 7.070. METHOD OF SERVICE OF PROCESS

Service of process shall be effected as provided by law or as provided by Florida Rule of Civil Procedure 1.070(a)–(h). Constructive service or substituted service of process may be effected as provided by law. Service of process on Florida residents only may also be effected by certified mail, return receipt signed by the defendant, or someone authorized to receive mail at the residence or principal place of business of the defendant. Either the clerk or an attorney of record may mail the certified mail, the cost of which is in addition to the filing fee.

RULE 7.080. SERVICE AND FILING OF PLEADINGS AND DOCUMENTS OTHER THAN STATEMENT OF CLAIM

(a) When Required. Copies of all pleadings and papers subsequent to the notice to appear, except applications for witness subpoenas and orders and judgments entered in open court, shall be served on each party. One against whom a default has been entered is entitled to be served only with pleadings asserting new or additional claims.

(b) How Made. When a party is represented by an attorney, service of papers other than the statement of claim and notice to appear shall be made on the attorney unless the court orders service to be made on the party. When an attorney is serving another attorney, service must be made in compliance with the Florida Rules of Judicial Administration. In all other instances, service must be made by delivering the paper to the party or the party's attorney, as the case may be, or by mailing it to the party's last known address.

(c) Filing. All original pleadings and papers shall be filed with the court either before service or immediately thereafter. The court may allow a copy to be substituted for the original of any document.

(d) Filing with the Court Defined. The filing of documents with the court as required by these rules is made by filing them with the clerk, except that the judge may permit the documents to be filed with the judge, in which event the judge shall note thereon the filing date and transmit them to the clerk, and the clerk shall file them as of the same date they were filed with the judge. Parties represented by an attorney must file documents in compliance with the electronic filing (e-filing) requirements set forth in the Florida Rules of Judicial Administration. Parties not represented by an attorney may file documents in compliance with the e-filing requirement if permitted by the Florida Rules of Judicial Administration.

(e) Certificate of Service.

(1) When any party or attorney in substance certifies:

"I certify that a copy hereof has been furnished to (here insert name or names and address or addresses) by (delivery) (mail) (e-mail if an attorney) on .....(date)......

_____

Party or party's attorney"

the certificate is prima facie proof of such service in compliance with all rules of court and law.

(2) When any paper is served by the clerk, a docket entry shall be made showing the mode and date of service. Such entry is sufficient proof of service without a separate certificate of service.

(f) When Unrepresented Party Fails to Show Service. If a party who is not represented by an attorney files a paper that does not show service of a copy on all other parties, the clerk shall serve a copy of it on all other parties.

RULE 7.090. APPEARANCE; DEFENSIVE PLEADINGS; TRIAL DATE

(a) Appearance. On the date and time appointed in the notice to appear, the plaintiff and defendant shall appear personally or by counsel.

(b) Notice to Appear; Pretrial Conference. The summons/notice to appear shall specify that the initial appearance shall be for a pretrial conference. The initial pretrial conference shall be set by the clerk not more than 50 days from the date of the filing of the action. The pretrial conference may be managed by nonjudicial personnel employed by or under contract with the court. Nonjudicial personnel must be subject to direct oversight by the court. A judge must be available to hear any motions or resolve any legal issues. At the pretrial conference, all of the following matters shall be considered:

(1) The simplification of issues.

(2) The necessity or desirability of amendments to the pleadings.

(3) The possibility of obtaining admissions of fact and of documents that avoid unnecessary proof.

(4) The limitations on the number of witnesses.

(5) The possibilities of settlement.

(6) Such other matters as the court in its discretion deems necessary. Form 7.322 shall and form 7.323 may be used in conjunction with this rule.

(c) Defensive Pleadings. Unless required by order of court, written pretrial motions and defensive pleadings are not necessary. If filed, copies of such pleadings shall be served on all other parties to the action at or prior to the pretrial conference or within such time as the court may designate. The filing of a motion or a defensive pleading shall not excuse the personal appearance of a party or attorney on the initial appearance date (pretrial conference).

(d) Trial Date. The court shall set the case for trial not more than 60 days from the date of the pretrial conference. At least 10 days' notice of the time of trial shall be given. The parties may stipulate to a shorter or longer time for setting trial with the approval of the court. This rule does not apply to actions to which chapter 51, Florida Statutes, applies.

(e) Waiver of Appearance at Pretrial Conference. Where all parties are represented by an attorney, counsel may agree to waive personal appearance at the initial pretrial conference, if a written agreement of waiver signed by all attorneys is presented to the court prior to or at the pretrial conference. The agreement shall contain a short statement of the disputed issues of fact and law, the number of witnesses expected to testify, an estimate of the time needed to try the case, and any stipulations of fact. The court shall forthwith set the case for trial within the time prescribed by these rules.

(f) Appearance at Mediation; Sanctions. In small claims actions, an attorney may appear on behalf of a party at mediation if the attorney has full authority to settle without further consultation. Unless otherwise ordered by the court, a nonlawyer representative may appear on behalf of a party to a small claims mediation if the representative has the party's signed written authority to appear and has full authority to settle without further consultation. In either event, the party need not appear in person. Mediation may take place at the pretrial conference. Whoever appears for a party must have full authority to settle. Failure to comply with this subdivision may result in the imposition [of] costs and attorney fees incurred by the opposing party.

(g) Agreement. Any agreements reached as a result of small claims mediation shall be written in the form of a stipulation. The stipulation may be entered as an order of the court.

RULE 7.100. COUNTERCLAIMS, SETOFFS, THIRD-PARTY COMPLAINTS, TRANSFER WHEN JURISDICTION EXCEEDED

(a) Compulsory Counterclaim. Any claim of the defendant against the plaintiff, arising out of the same transaction or occurrence which is the subject matter of the plaintiff's claim, shall be filed not less than 5 days prior to the initial appearance date (pretrial conference) or within such time as the court designates or it is deemed to be abandoned.

(b) Permissive Counterclaim. Any claim or setoff of the defendant against the plaintiff, not arising out of the transaction or occurrence which is the subject matter of the plaintiff's claim, may be filed not less than 5 days before the initial appearance date (pretrial conference) or within such time as the court designates, and tried, providing that such permissive claim is within the jurisdiction of the court.

(c) How Filed. Counterclaims and setoffs shall be filed in writing. If additional time is needed to prepare a defense, the court may continue the action.

(d) Transfer When beyond Jurisdiction. When a counterclaim or setoff exceeds the jurisdiction of the court, it shall be filed in writing before or at the hearing, and the action shall then be transferred to the court having jurisdiction thereof. As evidence of good faith, the counterclaimant shall deposit a sum sufficient to pay the filing fee in the court to which the case is to be transferred with the counterclaim, which shall be sent with the record to the court to which transferred. Failure to make the deposit waives the right to transfer.

(e) Third-Party Complaints. A defendant may cause a statement of claim to be served on a person not a party to the action who is or may be liable to the defendant for all or part of the plaintiff's claim against the defendant. A defendant must obtain leave of court on motion made at the initial appearance date (pretrial conference) and must file the third-party complaint within such time as the court may allow. The clerk shall schedule a supplemental pretrial conference, and on the date and time appointed in the notice to appear the third-party plaintiff and the third-party defendant shall appear personally or by counsel. If additional time is needed for the third-party defendant to prepare a defense, the court may continue the action. Any party may move to strike the third-party claim or for its severance or separate trial. When a counterclaim is asserted against the plaintiff, the plaintiff may bring in a third-party defendant under circumstances that would entitle a defendant to do so under this rule.

RULE 7.110. DISMISSAL OF ACTIONS

(a) Voluntary Dismissal; Effect Thereof.

(1) *By Parties.* Except in actions where property has been seized or is in the custody of the court, an action may be dismissed by the plaintiff without order of court (A) by the plaintiff informing the defendant and clerk of the dismissal before the trial date fixed in the notice to appear, or before retirement of the jury in a case tried before a jury or before submission of a nonjury case to the court for decision, or (B) by filing a stipulation of dismissal signed by all parties who have appeared in the action. Unless otherwise stated, the dismissal is without prejudice, except that a dismissal operates as an adjudication on the merits when a plaintiff has once dismissed in any court an action based on or including the same claim.

(2) *By Order of the Court; If Counterclaim.* Except as provided in subdivision (a)(1) of this rule, an action shall not be dismissed at a party's instance except upon order of the court and on such terms and conditions as the court deems proper. If a counterclaim has been made by the defendant before the plaintiff dismisses voluntarily, the action shall not be dismissed against the defendant's objections unless the counterclaim can remain pending for independent adjudication. Unless otherwise specified in the order, a dismissal under this subdivision is without prejudice.

(b) Involuntary Dismissal. Any party may move for dismissal of an action or of any claim against that party for failure of an adverse party to comply with these rules or any order of court. After a party seeking affirmative relief in an action has completed the presentation of evidence, any other party may move for a dismissal on the ground that upon the facts and the law the party seeking affirmative relief has shown no right to relief without waiving the right to offer evidence in the event the motion is not granted. The court may then determine them and render judgment against the party seeking affirmative relief or may decline to render any judgment until the close of all the evidence. Unless the court in its order for dismissal otherwise specifies, a dismissal under this subdivision and any dismissal not provided for in this rule, other than a dismissal for lack of jurisdiction or for improper venue or for lack of an indispensable party, operates as an adjudication on the merits.

(c) Dismissal of Counterclaim. The provisions of this rule apply to the dismissal of any counterclaim.

(d) Costs. Costs in any action dismissed under this rule shall be assessed and judgment for costs entered in that action. If a party who has once dismissed a claim in any court of this state commences an action based on or including the same claim against the same adverse party, the court shall make such order for the payment of costs of the claim previously dismissed as it may deem proper and shall stay the proceedings in the action until the party seeking affirmative relief has complied with the order.

(e) Failure to Prosecute. All actions in which it affirmatively appears that no action has been taken by filing of pleadings, order of court, or otherwise for a period of 6 months shall be dismissed by the court on its own motion or on motion of any interested person, whether a party to the action or not, after 30 days' notice to the parties, unless a stipulation staying the action has been filed with the court, or a stay order has been filed, or a party shows good cause in writin8g at least 5 days before the hearing on the motion why the action should remain pending.

RULE 7.130. CONTINUANCES AND SETTLEMENTS

(a) Continuances. A continuance may be granted only upon good cause shown. The motion for continuance may be oral, but the court may require that it be reduced to writing. The action shall be set again for trial as soon as practicable and the parties shall be given timely notice.

(b) Settlements. Settlements in full or by installment payments made by the parties out of the presence of the court are encouraged. The plaintiff shall notify the clerk of settlement, and the case may be dismissed or continued pending payments. Upon failure of a party to perform the terms of any stipulation or agreement for settlement of the claim before judgment, the court may enter appropriate judgment without notice upon the creditor's filing of an affidavit of the amount due.

RULE 7.135. SUMMARY DISPOSITION
At pretrial conference or at any subsequent hearing, if there is no triable issue, the court shall summarily enter an appropriate order or judgment.

RULE 7.140. TRIAL

(a) Time. The trial date shall be set by the court at the pretrial conference.

(b) Determination. Issues shall be settled and motions determined summarily.

(c) Pretrial. The pretrial conference should narrow contested factual issues. The case may proceed to trial with the consent of both parties.

(d) Settlement. At any time before judgment, the judge shall make an effort to assist the parties in settling the controversy by conciliation or compromise.

(e) Unrepresented Parties. In an effort to further the proceedings and in the interest of securing substantial justice, the court shall assist any party not represented by an attorney on:

(1) courtroom decorum;

(2) order of presentation of material evidence; and

(3) handling private information.

The court may not instruct any party not represented by an attorney on accepted rules of law. The court shall not act as an advocate for a party.

(f) How Conducted. The trial may be conducted informally but with decorum befitting a court of justice. The rules of evidence applicable to trial of civil actions apply but are to be liberally construed. At the discretion of the court, testimony of any party or witness may be presented over the telephone. Additionally, at the discretion of the court an attorney may represent a party or witness over the telephone without being physically present before the court. Any witness utilizing the privilege of testimony by telephone as permitted in this rule shall be treated for all purposes as a live witness, and shall not receive any relaxation of evidentiary rules or other special allowance. A witness may not testify over the telephone in order to avoid either the application of Florida's perjury laws or the rules of evidence.

RULE 7.150. JURY TRIALS

Jury trials may be had upon written demand of the plaintiff at the time of the commencement of the suit, or by the defendant within 5 days after service of notice of suit or at the pretrial conference, if any. Otherwise jury trial shall be deemed waived.

RULE 7.160. FAILURE OF PLAINTIFF OR BOTH PARTIES TO APPEAR

(a) Plaintiff. If plaintiff fails to appear on the initial appearance date (pretrial conference), or fails to appear at trial, the action may be dismissed for want of prosecution, defendant may proceed to trial on the merits, or the action may be continued as the judge may direct.

(b) Both Parties. If both parties fail to appear, the judge may continue the action or dismiss it for want of prosecution at that time or later as justice requires.

RULE 7.170. DEFAULT; JUDGMENT

(a) Default. If the defendant does not appear at the scheduled time, the plaintiff is entitled to a default to be entered by either the judge or clerk.

(b) Final Judgment. After default is entered, the judge shall receive evidence establishing the damages and enter judgment in accordance with the evidence and the law. The judge may inquire into and prevent abuses of venue prior to entering judgment.

RULE 7.175. MOTIONS FOR COSTS AND ATTORNEYS' FEES

Any party seeking a judgment taxing costs or attorneys' fees, or both, shall serve a motion no later than 30 days after filing of the judgment, including a judgment of dismissal, or the service of a notice of voluntary dismissal. In the event of a default judgment, no further motions are needed if costs or attorneys' fees, or both, were sought in the statement of claim.

RULE 7.180. MOTIONS FOR NEW TRIAL; TIME FOR; CONTENTS

(a) Time. A motion for new trial shall be filed not later than 10 days after return of verdict in a jury action or the date of filing of the judgment in a nonjury action. A timely motion may be amended to state new grounds at any time before it is disposed of in the discretion of the court.

(b) Determination. The motion shall set forth the basis with particularity. Upon examination of the motion, the court may find it without merit and deny it summarily, or may grant a hearing on it with notice.

(c) Grounds. All orders granting a new trial shall specify the specific grounds therefor. If such an order is appealed and does not state the specific grounds, the appellate court shall relinquish its jurisdiction to the trial court for entry of an order specifying the grounds for granting the new trial.

RULE 7.190. RELIEF FROM JUDGMENT OR ORDER; CLERICAL MISTAKES

(a) Clerical Mistakes. Clerical mistakes in judgments, orders, or other parts of the record and errors therein arising from oversight or omission may be corrected by the court at any time on its own initiative or on the motion of any party and after such notice, if any, as the court orders. During the pendency of an appeal, such mistakes may be so corrected before the record on appeal is docketed in the appellate court, and thereafter while the appeal is pending may be so corrected with leave of the appellate court.

(b) Mistakes; Inadvertence; Excusable Neglect; Newly Discovered Evidence; Fraud; etc. On motion and on such terms as are just, the court may relieve a party or a party's legal representative from a final judgment, order, or proceeding for the following reasons: (1) mistake, inadvertence, surprise, or excusable neglect; (2) newly discovered evidence which by due diligence could not have been discovered in time to move for a new trial or rehearing; (3)

fraud (whether heretofore denominated intrinsic or extrinsic), misrepresentation, or other misconduct of an adverse party; (4) the judgment is void; or (5) the judgment has been satisfied, released, or discharged or a prior judgment on which it is based has been reversed or otherwise vacated or it is no longer equitable that the judgment should have prospective application. The motion shall be made within a reasonable time, and for reasons (1), (2), and (3) not more than 1 year after the judgment, order, or proceeding was entered or taken. A motion under this subdivision does not affect the finality of a judgment or suspend its operation.

RULE 7.200. EXECUTIONS

Executions on judgments shall issue during the life of the judgment on the oral request of the party entitled to it or that party's attorney without praecipe. No execution or other final process shall issue until the judgment on which it is based has been rendered or within the time for serving a motion for new trial and, if a motion for new trial is timely served, until it is determined; provided execution or other final process may be issued on special order of the court at any time after judgment.

RULE 7.210. STAY OF JUDGMENT AND EXECUTION

(a) **Judgment or Execution or Levy Stayed.** When judgment is to be entered against a party, the judge may inquire and permit inquiry about the earnings and financial status of the party and has discretionary power to stay an entry of judgment or, if entered, to stay execution or levy on such terms as are just and in consideration of a stipulation on the part of the judgment debtor to make such payments as will ensure a periodic reduction of the judgment until it is satisfied.

(b) **Stipulation.** The judge shall note the terms of such stipulation in the file; the stipulation may be set out in the judgment or made a part of the judgment by reference to the stipulation made in open court.

(c) Execution. When judgment is entered and execution stayed pending payments, if the judgment debtor fails to pay the installment payments, the judgment creditor may have execution without further notice for the unpaid amount of the judgment upon filing an affidavit of the amount due.

(d) Oral Stipulations. Oral stipulations may be made in the presence of the court that upon failure of the judgment debtor to comply with any agreement, judgment may be entered or execution issued, or both, without further notice.

RULE 7.220. SUPPLEMENTARY PROCEEDINGS

Proceedings supplementary to execution may be had in accordance with proceedings provided by law or by the Florida Rules of Civil Procedure.

RULE 7.221. HEARING IN AID OF EXECUTION

(a) Use of Form 7.343. In any final judgment, the judge shall include the Enforcement Paragraph of form 7.340 if requested by the prevailing party or attorney. In addition to the forms of discovery available to the judgment creditor under Fla. R. Civ. P. 1.560, the judge, at the request of the judgment creditor or the judgment creditor's attorney, shall order a judgment debtor to complete form 7.343 within 30 days of the order or other such reasonable time determined by the court. If the judgment debtor fails to obey the order, Fla. R. Civ. P. Form 1.982 may be used in conjunction with this subdivision of this rule.

(b) Purpose of Hearing. The judge, at the request of the judgment creditor, shall order a judgment debtor to appear at a hearing in aid of execution at a time certain 30 or more days from the date of entry of a judgment for the purpose of inquiring of the judgment debtor under oath as to earnings, financial status, and any assets available in excess of exemptions to be applied towards satisfaction of judgment. The provisions of this subdivision of this rule shall only apply to a judgment creditor who is a natural person and was not represented by an attorney prior to judgment. Forms 7.342, 7.343, and 7.344 shall be used in connection with this subdivision of this rule.

RULE 7.230. APPELLATE REVIEW

Review of orders and judgments of the courts governed by these rules shall be prosecuted in accordance with the Florida Rules of Appellate Procedure.

Clerks of Court (Mailing Addresses and Websites as of July 2013)

ALACHUA COUNTY
Clerk: Buddy Irby
201 E. University Ave., Gainesville, FL 32601
Telephone (352) 374-3636
http://www.alachuacounty.us/Depts/Clerk/Pages/Clerk.aspx

BAKER COUNTY
Clerk: Al Fraser
339 E. Macclenny Avenue, Suite 113
Macclenny, FL 32063
Telephone (904) 259-8113, press 0
http://bakercountyfl.org/clerk/

BAY COUNTY
Clerk: Bill Kinsaul
P.O. Box 2269, Panama City, FL 32402
or 300 East 4th Street, Panama City, FL 32401
Telephone (850) 747-5222
http://www.baycoclerk.com/

BRADFORD COUNTY
Clerk: Ray Norman
P.O. Drawer B, Starke, FL 32091
or 945 N. Temple Ave., Starke, FL 32091
Telephone (904) 966-6280
http://www.bradfordcountyfl.gov/clerkIndex.html

BREVARD COUNTY
Clerk: Scott Ellis
P.O. Box 999, Titusville, FL 32781-0999
or 400 South Street, Titusville, FL 32780
Telephone (321) 637-2017
http://brevardclerk.us/

BROWARD COUNTY
Clerk: Howard C. Forman
201 S. E. 6th Street, Room 136
Ft. Lauderdale, FL 33301
Telephone (954) 831-7019
http://www.clerk-17th-flcourts.org/ClerkWebSite/Welcome2.aspx

CALHOUN COUNTY
Clerk: Carla Hand
20859 Central Avenue E., Room 130
Blountstown, FL 32424
Telephone (850) 674-4545
http://www.calhounclerk.com/

CHARLOTTE COUNTY
Clerk: Barbara T. Scott
350 East Marion Ave.
Punta Gorda, FL 33950

Telephone (941) 505-4716
http://www.co.charlotte.fl.us/Default.aspx

CITRUS COUNTY
Clerk: Angela Vick
110 North Apopka Avenue
Inverness, FL 34450-4299
Telephone (352) 341-6414
http://www.clerk.citrus.fl.us/

CLAY COUNTY
Clerk: Tara Green
P.O. Box 698, Green Cove Springs, FL 32043
or 825 North Orange Ave., Green Cove Springs, FL 32043
Telephone (904) 284-6317
http://clayclerk.com/default.html

COLLIER COUNTY
Clerk: Dwight E. Brock
P.O. Box 413044, Naples, FL 34101-3044
or 3315 Tamiami Trail East, Suite 102,
Naples, FL 34112-5324
Telephone (239) 252-2646
http://www.clerk.collier.fl.us/

COLUMBIA COUNTY
Clerk: P. Dewitt Cason
P.O. Box 2069, Lake City, FL 32056
or 173 N.E. Hernando Ave., Lake City, FL 32055
Telephone (386) 758-1041 or (386) 758-1191
http://www.columbiaclerk.com/

DESOTO COUNTY
Clerk: Mitzie W. McGavic
115 East Oak Street, Arcadia, FL 34266-2401
Telephone (863) 993-4876
http://www.desotoclerk.com/

DIXIE COUNTY
Clerk: Dana Johnson
P.O. Box 1206, Cross City, FL 32628-1206
or 214 N.E. 351 Hwy., Suite M Cross City, FL 32628-1206
Telephone (352) 498-1200
http://www.dixieclerk.com/

DUVAL COUNTY
Clerk: Ronnie Fussell
501 West Adams Street, Room 2356
Jacksonville, FL 32202
Telephone (904) 255-2000
http://www.duvalclerk.com/ccWebsite/

ESCAMBIA COUNTY
Clerk: Pamela Childers
P.O. Box 333, Pensacola, FL 32591-0333
or 190 Governmental Street
Pensacola, FL 32502
Telephone (850) 595-4310
http://www.escambiaclerk.com/clerk/index.aspx

FLAGLER COUNTY
Clerk: Gail Wadsworth
The Kim C. Hammond Justice Center
1769 East Moody Blvd., Bldg. #1, Bunnell, FL 32110

Telephone (386) 313-4409
http://www.flaglerclerk.com/

FRANKLIN COUNTY
Clerk: Marcia Johnson
33 Market St., Ste. 203, Apalachicola, FL 32320
Telephone (850) 653-8861 ext. 103
http://www.franklinclerk.com/

GADSDEN COUNTY
Clerk: Nicholas Thomas
P.O. Box 1649, Quincy, FL 32353-1649
or 10 East Jefferson Street, Quincy, FL 32351-2406
Telephone (850) 875-8601 ext. 224
http://www.gadsdenclerk.com/

GILCHRIST COUNTY
Clerk: Todd Newton
3P.O. Box 37, Trenton, FL 32693
or 112 S. Main St., Trenton, FL 32693
Telephone (352) 463-3170
http://www.gilchristclerk.com/

GLADES COUNTY
Clerk: Sandra Brown
P.O. Box 10, Moore Haven, FL 33471
or 500 Avenue J, Suite 102, Moore Haven, FL 33471
Telephone (863) 946-6010
http://www.gladesclerk.com/

GULF COUNTY
Clerk: Rebecca Norris
1000 Cecil G. Costin, Sr. Blvd., Rm. 148

Port St. Joe, FL 32456
Telephone (850) 229-6112
http://www.gulfclerk.com/

HAMILTON COUNTY
Clerk: W. Greg Godwin
207 N.E. 1st Street, Room 106, Jasper, FL 32052
Telephone (386) 792-1288
http://www.hamiltoncountyflorida.com/cd_clerk.aspx

HARDEE COUNTY
Clerk: Victoria L. Rogers
P.O. Drawer 1749, Wauchula, FL 33873
or 417 West Main Street, Room 202, Wauchula, FL 33873
Telephone (863) 773-4174
http://www.hardeeclerk.com/

HENDRY COUNTY
Clerk: Barbara Butler
P.O. Box 1760, LaBelle, FL 33975
or 25 Hickpochee Ave., LaBelle, FL 33935
Telephone (863) 675-5217
http://www.hendryclerk.org/

HERNANDO COUNTY
Clerk: Don Barbee
20 North Main Street, Room 130, Brooksville, FL 34601
Telephone - Office (352) 754-4201
http://hernandoclerk.com/

HIGHLANDS COUNTY
Clerk: Robert Germaine
590 South Commerce Avenue, Sebring, FL 33870-3867

Telephone (863) 402-6564
http://www.hcclerk.org/home.aspx

HILLSBOROUGH COUNTY
Clerk: Pat Frank
P.O. Box 1110, Tampa, FL 33601
or County Center, 13th Floor., 601 E. Kennedy Blvd.
Tampa, FL 33602
Telephone (813) 276-8100
http://www.hillsclerk.com/

HOLMES COUNTY
Clerk: Kyle Hudson
P.O. Box 397, Bonifay, FL 32425
or 201 N. Oklahoma St.. Bonifay, FL 32425
Telephone (850) 547-1100
http://www.holmesclerk.com/

INDIAN RIVER COUNTY
Clerk: Jeffrey R. Smith
P.O. Box 1028, Vero Beach, FL 32961-1028
or 2000 16th Avenue, Vero Beach, FL 32960
Telephone (772) 770-5185
http://www.clerk.indian-river.org/

JACKSON COUNTY
Clerk: Dale Rabon Guthrie
P.O. Drawer 510, Marianna, FL 32447
or 4445 Lafayette Street, Marianna, FL 32446
Telephone (850) 482-9552
http://www.jacksonclerk.com/

JEFFERSON COUNTY
Clerk: Kirk Reams
1 Courthouse Circle, Monticello, FL 32344
Telephone (850) 342-0218 ext. 232
http://jeffersonclerk.com/

LAFAYETTE COUNTY
Clerk: Ricky Lyons
P.O. Box 88, Mayo, FL 32066
or 120 West Main Street, Mayo, FL 32066
Telephone (386) 294-1600
http://www.lafayetteclerk.com/

LAKE COUNTY
Clerk: Neil Kelly
P.O. Box 7800, Tavares, FL 32778-7800
or 550 West Main Street, Tavares, FL 32778-3115
Telephone (352) 742-4100
http://www.lakecountyclerk.org/

LEE COUNTY
Clerk: Linda Doggett
P. O. Box 2469, Ft. Myers, FL 33902
or 2075 Dr. Martin Luther King Jr. Blvd., Ft. Myers, FL 33901
Telephone (239) 533-5000
http://www.leeclerk.org/

LEON COUNTY
Clerk: Bob Inzer
P.O. Box 726, Tallahassee, FL 32302
or 301 South Monroe Street, Suite 100, Tallahassee, FL 32301
Telephone (850) 577-4000
http://www.clerk.leon.fl.us/

LEVY COUNTY
Clerk: Danny J. Shipp
355 Court Street, Bronson, FL 32621
Telephone (352) 486-5266
http://levyclerk.com/

LIBERTY COUNTY
Clerk: Kathleen Brown
P.O. Box 399, Bristol, FL 32321
Telephone (850) 643-2215 or (850) 643-2237
http://www.libertyclerk.com/

MADISON COUNTY
CLERK: TIM SANDERS
P.O. Box 237, Madison, FL 32341-0237
or 125 SW Range Avenue, Madison, FL 32340
Telephone (850) 973-1500 or (850) 973-8000
http://www.madisonclerk.com/

MANATEE COUNTY
Clerk: R. B. "Chips" Shore
P.O. Box 25400, Bradenton, FL 34206
or 1115 Manatee Avenue W., Bradenton, FL 34205
Telephone (941) 749-1800
http://www.manateeclerk.com/

MARION COUNTY
Clerk: David R. Ellspermann
P.O. Box 1030, Ocala, FL 34478
110 N. W. 1st Avenue, Ocala, FL 34475
Telephone (352) 671-5604
http://www.marioncountyclerk.org/

MARTIN COUNTY
Clerk: Carolyn Timmann
P.O. Drawer 9016, Stuart, FL 34995
or 100 E. Ocean Blvd., Stuart, FL 34994
Telephone (772) 288-5736
http://clerk-web.martin.fl.us/ClerkWeb/

MIAMI-DADE COUNTY
Clerk: Harvey Ruvin
73 West Flagler Street, Suite 242, Miami, FL 33130
Telephone (305) 349-7333
http://www.miami-dadeclerk.com/

MONROE COUNTY
Clerk: Amy Heavilin
P.O. Box 1980, Key West, FL 33040
or 500 Whitehead Street, Key West, FL 33040
Telephone (305) 295-3130
https://gov.propertyinfo.com/fl-monroe/

NASSAU COUNTY
Clerk: John Crawford
76347 Veterans Way, Suite 456, Yulee, FL 32097
Telephone (904) 548-4600
http://www.nassauclerk.org/

OKALOOSA COUNTY
Clerk: Don Howard
101 E. James Lee B8lvd., Suite 105, Crestview FL 32536
Telephone (850) 689-5000 ext 4301
http://www.clerkofcourts.cc/

OKEECHOBEE COUNTY
Clerk: Sharon Robertson
312 N.W. 3rd Street, Suite 101, Okeechobee, FL 34972
Telephone (863) 763-2131
http://www.clerk.co.okeechobee.fl.us/

ORANGE COUNTY
Interim Clerk: Colleen Reilly
P.O. Box 4994, Orlando, FL 32802-4994
or 425 N. Orange Ave., Suite 2110, Orlando, FL 32801
Telephone (407) 836-2000
http://www.myorangeclerk.com/

OSCEOLA COUNTY
Clerk: Armando Ramirez
2 Courthouse Square, Suite 2000, Kissimmee, FL 34741
Telephone (407) 742-3708
http://www.osceolaclerk.com/

PALM BEACH COUNTY
Clerk: Sharon Bock
P.O. Box 229, West Palm Beach, FL 33402
or 301 North Olive, 9th Floor, West Palm Beach, FL 33401
Telephone (561) 355-2996
http://www.mypalmbeachclerk.com/

PASCO COUNTY
Clerk: Paula O'neil
7530 Little Road, Suite 106, New Port Richey, FL 34654
P.O. Box 338, New Port Richey, FL 34656-0338
Telephone (727) 847-8199 - New Port Richey
Telephone (352) 523-2411 Ext. 8199 - Dade City
http://www.pascoclerk.com/

PINELLAS COUNTY
Clerk: Ken Burke
315 Court Street, Room 400, Clearwater, FL 33756
Telephone: (727) 464-3341
http://www.pinellasclerk.org/

POLK COUNTY
Clerk: Stacy Butterfield
P.O. Box 9000, Drawer CC-1, Bartow, FL 33831
or 255 N. Broadway, Bartow, FL 33830
Telephone (863) 534-4000
http://www.polkcountyclerk.net/

PUTNAM COUNTY
Clerk: Tim Smith
P.O. Box 758, Palatka, FL 32178-0758
or 410 St. Johns Avenue, Palatka, FL 32177
Telephone (386) 326-7600
http://www.putnam-fl.com/coc/

ST. JOHNS COUNTY
Clerk: Cheryl Strickland
4010 Lewis Speedway, St. Augustine, FL 32084
Telephone (904) 819-3600
http://www.co.st-johns.fl.us/Const-Officers/Clerk-of-Court/index.htm

ST. LUCIE COUNTY
Clerk: Joe Smith
201 South Indian River Drive, Fort Pierce, FL 34950
Telephone (772) 462-6900
http://www.stlucieclerk.com/

SANTA ROSA COUNTY
Clerk: Donald Spencer
P.O. Box 472, Milton, FL 32572
or 6495 Caroline St., Suite A, Milton, FL 32570
Telephone (850) 981-5583
http://www.santarosaclerk.com/

SARASOTA COUNTY
Clerk: Karen E. Rushing
P.O. Box 3079, Sarasota, FL 34230-3079
or Sarasota County Courthouse, 2000 Main St.,
Sarasota, FL 34237
Telephone (941) 861-7400
http://www.sarasotaclerk.com/

SEMINOLE COUNTY
Clerk: Maryanne Morse
P.O. Box 8099, Sanford, FL 32772-8099
or 301 N. Park Avenue, Sanford, FL 32771-1243
Telephone (407) 665-4330
http://www.seminoleclerk.org/

SUMTER COUNTY
Clerk: Gloria R. Hayward
P.O. Box 2587, Bushnell, FL 33513
or 215 E. McCollum Avenue, Bushnell, FL 33513
Telephone (352) 569-6600
http://www.sumterclerk.com/index.cfm/home

SUWANNEE COUNTY
Clerk: Barry Baker
200 South Ohio Ave./Dr. MLK, Jr. Ave., Live Oak, FL 32064

Telephone (386) 362-0526
http://www.suwclerk.org/

TAYLOR COUNTY
Clerk: Annie Mae Murphy
P.O. Box 620, Perry, FL 32348
or 108 N. Jefferson Street, Suite 102, Perry, FL 32347
Telephone (850) 838-3506
http://www.taylorclerk.com/

UNION COUNTY
Clerk: Kellie Hendricks-Connell
55 West Main Street
Union County Courthouse, Room 103
Lake Butler, FL 32054
Telephone (386) 496-3711
http://www.unionclerk.com/

VOLUSIA COUNTY
Clerk: Diane M. Matousek
P.O. Box 6043, Deland, FL 32721-6043
or 101 N. Alabama Ave., Deland, FL 32724
Telephone (386) 822-5710 or (386) 736-5915
http://www.clerk.org/

WAKULLA COUNTY
Clerk: Brent X. Thurmond
3056 Crawfordville Highway, Crawfordville, FL 32327
Telephone (850) 926-0905
http://www.wakullaclerk.com/

WALTON COUNTY
Clerk: Alex Alford
P.O. Box 1260, DeFuniak Springs, FL 32435-1260
or 571 U.S. Hwy. 90 East, DeFuniak Springs, FL 32433
Telephone (850) 951-7263
http://clerkofcourts.co.walton.fl.us/

WASHINGTON COUNTY
Clerk: Linda Hayes Cook
P.O. Box 647, Chipley, FL 32428
or 1293 Jackson Ave., Chipley, FL 32428
Telephone (850) 638-6289
http://www.washingtonclerk.com/

ABOUT THE AUTHORS

Kurt E. Lee has been a Florida trial attorney since 1993 and a Board Certified Business Litigation Lawyer since 2002. Kurt graduated from The George Washington University, cum laude, as a Philosophy major and, then, graduated, again with honors, from the University of Florida College of Law. Kurt has written articles for The Florida Bar *Journal*, The Florida Real Property, Probate, and Trust Section's *ActionLine*, and other media outlets. Kurt is a member of Supreme Court of Florida Committee on Standard Jury Instructions - Contract and Business Cases and is the managing partner of Kurt E. Lee, PL. For more information about Kurt or to contact him, please visit www.kurtelee.com.

Timothy W. Sobczak has been a Florida trial attorney since 2010. Tim received his Bachelor's Degree from the University of Central Florida in 2005 and his Juris Doctor from the University of Florida College of Law in 2010, cum laude, where he was an assistant editor of the Florida Law Review. Tim has written articles for The Florida Bar *Journal* and the *Florida Law Review*. Tim is an associate at the law firm of Dean Mead and practices in its Orlando office. For more information about Tim or to contact him, please visit www.deanmead.com.